PROTESTANTS AGAINST POVERTY

Contributions in American History

Series Editor
STANLEY I. KUTLER
University of Wisconsin

PROTESTANTS AGAINST POVERTY

Boston's Charities, 1870–1900

Nathan Irvin Huggins
Foreword by Oscar Handlin

*CONTRIBUTIONS IN
AMERICAN HISTORY*
Number Nine

Greenwood Publishing Corporation
WESTPORT, CONNECTICUT

Library of Congress Catalog Card Number: 70-105980
SBN: 8371-3307-6

Greenwood Publishing Corporation
51 Riverside Avenue, Westport, Connecticut 06880

Greenwood Publishers Ltd.
London, England

Printed in the United States of America

KATHRYN HUGGINS TREADWELL (1925–1957)
WHO WAS ESSENTIAL TO ME

Contents

Foreword

Americans tend to take for granted the institutions of modern philanthropy which play so important a part in the life of their society. Few are aware of the way in which the modes of assisting the dependent developed in the past or of the influence still exerted by earlier efforts to deal with the problems of the needy. The welfare agencies of 1970 did not always exist; they would have seemed strange even a century ago. They appeared at a special stage in the development of western society, and they took a unique form in the United States because of distinctive attitudes toward the responsibilities of the community to those of its members who could not support themselves.

In every society, of course, there were people who could not make a go of it. The orphans without parents, the aged without sustaining children, the ill and the incompetent, the landless, the people without skills, and those who had no strength to earn their own livelihood all needed help. But initially, the responsibility for providing such assistance rested upon the family. The obligation was seen as one of blood and was recognized by—often confined to—the clan which

was held together by kinship. In some sense, acceptance of
this type of responsibility persisted into modern times and
still exists.

In the more recent past, however, the sense of obligation
broadened to encompass the whole community. In Europe,
the village in which the peasant lived underwrote the responsibilities of the family and bore the burdens when kins-
men could not. In more complicated places, like the medieval
or early modern cities, the guilds and fraternities developed
schemes of self-help by which the individuals who needed
support could get it. And specialized groups within the society like religious or ethnic minorities accepted the obligation of providing their own resources to aid their members.

Only with the appearance of the national state in very
modern times did the sense of responsibility acquire still
broader dimensions. Now care of the dependent became an
aspect of the government's exercise of power to maintain
order. The existence of rogues, vagabonds, idle persons, beggars, and unsightly or disturbing individuals was a nuisance
and a threat; and the state undertook to control such people
either by getting them out of the way into institutions or
by some alternative form of relief. This was the background
in England, and in western Europe in general, in the period
in which the colonists began to lay the basis of their own
institutions. By and large, the colonists aimed to transplant
to the New World the same pattern of family, community,
and state obligations they had known in the Old World.

Significantly, the point at which the political revolution
of 1776 separated the United States from Britain was also
a point at which the basic conception of philanthropy
changed. The traditional attitude of the past had valued
the giving of alms as an act of charity. The dominant Christian view until then had defined the act of charity, not pri-
marily as a means of helping those who needed help, but
rather as a means by which the virtuous exercised one of

their religious faculties. The poor and dependent existed so that the well-to-do and the able would be in a position to demonstrate their own goodness. Even the eighteenth-century Enlightenment, which had a marked influence upon the Americans as upon Europeans, merely secularized this view. Philanthropy became an aspect of benevolence, by which the humane and cultivated man demonstrated his generous sentiments. But that conception still emphasized the value of the act of assistance to the donor rather than to the recipient of charity.

The Revolutionary era began to reverse that traditional emphasis. Men who believed in progress and in the possibility of improvement saw the dependent in a new light. The growing humanitarianism of the period rested upon a deep faith in human nature, indeed it embraced a belief in the perfectibility of mankind. From that point of view, the person who required help was a challenge; and assistance was not so much charity—an occasion on which the benevolent showed their goodness—as the means by which society acted to improve itself.

It would take well over a century for the new understanding to transform the old institutions of philanthropy. Assistance that reflected broad humanitarian concerns had to pass beyond the ties of blood and kinship to involve the whole society. It had to break out of the restricted circles of the small community. And it had to be administered by voluntary means as well as by the power of the state.

Americans of the nineteenth century, therefore, faced the problems not simply of adapting European institutions to the conditions of the New World, but also those of implementing the new concepts of mutual obligation that the Revolutionary era had nurtured. It would take a long and complex development to move beyond the vague rhetoric of progress to the actual creation of the necessary forms of aid.

The difficulties were less imposing in rural areas than in the city. The large, impersonal city was a setting in which thousands of unrelated individuals floated about without the links that made fruitful association possible. There too a dynamic but unstable and unregulated economy generated a host of dependent people—the poor, the idle, the ill. The city was also a dangerous place. Life there was laden with uncertainty, and the family was rarely in a position to perform the services it had formerly rendered. The result was an impression of chaos and a fear of forces that individuals could not control.

These problems were dramatically apparent in Boston. Until the revolution the city had grown up as a homogeneous community very conscious of and sensitive to humanitarian sentiments. In the second quarter of the nineteenth century, however, it suffered a serious shock as a result of mass immigration and of the beginnings of industrialization. It then suddenly faced the problems of applying to practice the concepts of humanitarian philanthropy that it had inherited from the eighteenth century. Its citizens had to struggle to develop forms which would make possible voluntary, yet scientific, assistance. The problems they encountered in doing so and the extent to which they succeeded and failed are the dominant themes of Professor Huggins's careful study.

OSCAR HANDLIN

April 1970

Acknowledgments

Small books gather a disproportionate share of obligations. So it is with this one. I will be unable to mention on these pages all those deserving of my thanks. Many who have helped me in large and small ways will know that my gratitude abides although their names will not appear here.

The John Hay Whitney Opportunity Fellowships and the Jessie Smith Noyes Foundation helped support my research, thus exemplifying that philanthropic spirit which is the subject of this study. My work was eased by the cordial cooperation of the staffs of several libraries: Widener, Houghton, the Massachusetts Historical Society, and Simmons College. The staffs of the Boston Family Service Association, the Boston Children's Service Association, and the Boston Visiting Nurses' Association were very helpful to me in opening the records of the various nineteenth century societies long since incorporated into these modern conglomerate organizations. This study would have been impossible without the generous help of the managers of these associations.

There are other, more personal, obligations which language can neither repay nor fully explain. Mrs. Eva Jacobs alone will know why her name must appear here and why this book would never have appeared without her. Casual Sunday talks with Howard Thurman, while watching televised morality plays in the guise of professional football, unraveled theological knots. In those struggles between Good and Evil, Evil, true to life, triumphed more often than not. Several contemporaries and friends gave from their own work to listen to thoughts about mine: Stephen W. Booth, Valentin Rabe, Richard Sewell, Van Perkins, and Stephan Thernstrom. Corinne Freeman Smith's fine intelligence and critical eye considered a rough typescript, and her suggestions were indispensable to the refinements that have since appeared.

I am pleased that my name will add to the lengthening list of historians indebted to our teacher, Oscar Handlin. He has helped us all to see American history and social history in fresh ways. More, he has honored us through his respect for our individual insights and imaginations.

Of course, I alone am responsible for what appears on these pages. No one I have mentioned here should be embarrassed because I have done that.

PROTESTANTS AGAINST POVERTY

Abbreviations

1

Introduction

HISTORIANS had already turned their attention to the study of America's treatment of the poor before it had become fashionable to write of "the other America" and the "war on poverty."[1] Because America's concept of poverty as a pervasive social issue matured in the late nineteenth century, these works necessarily have taken that period as a point of departure; several, however, have focused on the early decades of this century. Resonating the spirit of those years, these works have assumed that the reforms they discuss were truly progressive, liberating, and constructive responses to the challenge of poverty. While I do not completely discount that assumption, I think that this book discovers a deeply conservative (if not reactionary) element in the efforts of charity workers to address the problems of their time. A few years ago it was easy to find hope and comfort in progressive remedies and programs designed to ameliorate poverty. Easier, that is, than it is today. The various skirmishes in the "war on poverty" have served mainly to impress upon us the enormity of the conflict and poverty's relative unresponsiveness to all past palliatives. Our cities' seeming futility in affecting the lives of the poor draws us more urgently than ever to the last decades of the nineteenth century when humane Americans first felt themselves overwhelmed.

Like many Americans in 1894, William Dean Howells was deeply disturbed about the social conditions in the United States, so he fictionalized a Mr. Homos from the mythical Altruria to visit this country and say what Howells thought was wrong. What shocked Mr. Homos most was the social alienation of Americans. Private enterprise and materialism had resulted in the exploitation of man by man and the great disparities of poverty and affluence, penury amidst plenty. And he found most appalling the attitudes of the wealthy, whose complacency and self-satisfaction suffered the most astringent interpretation of Christian obligation. After all, as they saw it, a system requiring individual initiative had permitted their own success; sentimental succor to the poor could only serve to undermine the system that had allowed them to thrive.

A Traveler From Altruria was only one of that period's many efforts of imagination which attempted to adjudge the American present in terms of Christian principles presumed to be shared by all. Howells had been influenced by Edward Bellamy's *Looking Backward* (1888), but there was also W. T. Stead's *If Christ Came to Chicago* (1894), C. M. Sheldon's *In His Steps* (1897), and Edward Everett Hale's *If Jesus Came to Boston* (1894), and the list is long. These efforts merely attest to the suspicion among many that the promise of American life, at least as it had resulted in material progress and wealth, was widely removed from God's plan. Somehow the voluntary social arrangements which had always been assumed to ameliorate human suffering and want through the stewardship of the affluent no longer worked. It seemed pitifully inadequate in the severe economic crises of the 1870s, 1880s, and 1890s. Like Mr. Homos, many men focused their attention on charity, because tradition told them it was the very life-stuff of community. And everyone understood that what was in jeopardy of disintegration was the genuine community which held itself together by mutual obligation.

The causes of community crisis were not difficult to discover. Cities had grown enormously in the fifty years or so from the end of the Mexican War, when the United States had achieved full continental growth. They had grown in population because of the accelerating shift from agriculture to industry and finance as the main foci of American economic life. New and fertile western lands made farming a narrow, competitive enterprise for easterners, so many moved —displaced as farms went out of production and as they became convinced that new opportunities were in the cities. If there was a better chance to be found in the urban setting, industry provided it. But it beckoned the foreign as well as the native migrant, depending as it did on large concentrations of labor from which it could draw at the cheapest wage. Thus, it was not simply greater numbers that threatened community in the cities, but urban populations became more radically heterogeneous as the waves of foreign immigrants, which had begun early in the century, swelled to tidal proportions in the decades following the Civil War. And the newer waves brought fewer of the familiar Britons and northern Europeans and more of the stranger folk from the South and the East of Europe.

When men viewed their burgeoning cities, they saw the community problem as threefold. Few of the newer people shared the values, language, and traditions common to American life. Their greater numbers also encouraged the impersonality of bureaucratic and institutional devices. And finally, the growing disparity between rich and poor (where they lived and how they lived), as the progress of the few was overbalanced by the poverty and apparent helplessness of the many, made common experience and communication problematic. Concerned contemporaries, regardless of how they might imagine the problems would be solved, would recognize these symptoms of community malaise. Many would recall a time that had passed (real or fancied) when all men knew one another and could relate as men—able to adjudge each other's strengths and weaknesses of character—rather than as elements of impersonal conglomerates, generated by social and group interest. Especially as one considered ethical problems within the social context, it appeared that cities in the last three decades of the nineteenth century were depriving men of the means to live naturally with one another as Christians. Some hoped a contrivance might be found to return human social experience to true principles.

Like cities, modern industry seemed to have shattered traditional relationships. The increased incorporation and the growing concentration of industry made the personal, human relationship between management and labor impossible. The corporation as a legal personality was the entity for whom business decisions were properly made. Did the corporation have ethical and moral obligations over and above what the law required? A Thoreau might have said, the corporation had no soul; therefore it acted for the sake of expediency, not Christian obligation. The directors served the legal creature, not their ethical selves, their men, or their communities.

Similarly, as industrial plants became bigger, even the indulged fiction of individual workmen was swallowed up into the reality of massive labor pools. Industrial concentration also meant the interdependence of interrelated industries; each economic crisis was more intensive and more extensive than the one that had gone before. Individuals became the playthings of impersonal business cycles, which refused to honor one's industry, frugality, and those other achievement virtues that were traditional to . American life. Whatever other community sense industry might have had was now diffused as the economy became more national; the community, the locality, the region had less claim on the businesses within it as those enterprises became more tied to national markets and sources of finance. The workmen's natural answer to this impersonalized industry was a concentration of their own into labor unions. Labor's early efforts to organize reflected their dismay at community disintegration. Even the Knights of Labor hoped to join all producers (workers and managers) in a common organization; they resisted the wage system which treated labor as any other commodity, and they experimented with producer cooperatives which were designed to end the differences between capital and labor by fusing them as one. By the end of the century, however, most organized labor had succumbed to the notion that collective (impersonal) action in the group's interest was the only defense against an industrial system where personal worth had no value except as it was sustained by aggregate power. It is of little wonder, then, that men of deep Christian conviction should be concerned about a community where power and factional interests were replacing ethical judgments and personal religious obligation as the basis of human interaction.

Like William Dean Howells, many of those who tried to imagine new directions for the reestablishment of effective community relations placed ethical and Christian principles first, even before the presumed laws of the economic system. Bellamy and Howells envisioned an "evolution" which might transform a society tyrannized by trusts into a benevolent, humane community which would serve the individual through serving the general will. Or Sheldon's very popular *In His Steps* transformed a fictional community simply by having everyone follow the teachings of Jesus, even to making unbusinesslike decisions. More sophisticated studies, like those of the economist Simon Patten (trained in the strongly ethical German historical school), urged the reconception of

America as a society of abundance rather than one of scarc-
ity in order that economic consideration might be shifted
from concerns over wages, prices, and profits to that of
equitable distribution.[2] Such men knew that a system that
rested upon individual enterprise and self-interest and assumed that an "invisible hand" would serve the community,
could not properly emphasize personal ethics nor bind men
together in mutual benefit.

Not all of those deeply concerned with community disintegration, however, would have found the economic system
at fault. What could be more natural and right than a social
arrangement where men succeeded or failed through their
own talent and luck? It had brought the nation far. And
while there were growing numbers of dependent poor and
alarming increases of crime and delinquency, was it not better to force people to achieve their manhood through a system of independence than to indulge their helplessness? Certainly, cities were too big and industrial relations too problematic to make for community cohesion. Scale alone exacer-
bated crime and dependency and weakened men's ability to
abate them. Statistics—a sign of mass dimensions—became a
new device to discover the magnitude of social problems.
Social science (at least a scientific method applied to society)
was employed in place of sentiment in the assessment of social problems and the design of their solutions. If numbers
and conditions made impossible informed behavior based on
personal observation, then exactitude and an even better
intelligence might come through statistics and improved
methods. If the community was in jeopardy, threatening
order and continued progress, was not the proper thing to
contrive new means to guarantee tradition under these new
circumstances?

Those reformers who considered the faults of dependency
to be in the character of individuals turned their attention
to the reform of charities, hoping to assure that only honest

need and uplift would be served. After 1870, the Charity Organization Movement, the major contrivance of these charity reformers, became something of a fad; most American cities had agencies which shared in the movement. In 1893, Charles D. Kellogg could report to the National Conference on Charities and Corrections that in the twenty years from the initial organization in Buffalo, ninety-two cities in the United States and Canada had charitable associations which ascribed in some rough way to reform principles.[3] Those principles were broad enough to permit wide variation in practice. The reformers wanted to include all relief outside of institutions (outdoor relief as they called it) under the control of a single reform-inspired agency, work toward the reduction and total abolition of such relief, and use "friendly visitors" and other provident enterprises to help redeem the poor and to lift them from their dependency. By central control, frauds could be detected and exposed, and data could be gathered to help in the ultimate social amelioration.

Of course, the Charity Organization Movement was a reform of private philanthropy, but it reflected similar reform efforts in public administration of aid to dependent classes. The two sectors were intimately related. The reformers wanted to end street begging, crack down on vagrancy, and end the granting of all public aid to those who were not institutionalized or otherwise helpless. Reformers in private agencies, therefore, worked as much through their political and social influence to change public practices as they did through the organizations they served and created.

Like private charities, public welfare agencies underwent profound changes in the last thirty years of the century. The reform was national, but most states took their lead from Massachusetts, which had established a state board of charities as early as 1863. Local peculiarities and growing centralization of state government made the conventional legislative visiting committees and grand juries inadequate to oversee properly the vast and complex network of services that the states were required to provide. Under the leadership of that venerable reformer, Samuel Gridley Howe, and with the forceful administration of Franklin B. Sanborn, the Massachusetts State Board of Charities served as a model to others. It required all eleemosynary organizations requiring tax-free status to register with the Board and supply it with information about its activities. In this way, the Board became an important information resource in a time that was conscious about the need for data. Through its leadership, separate commissions were established to supervise the state's penal institutions and insane asylums. This became the pattern in the reform of public welfare throughout the country. Other states followed: in 1867 New York and Ohio, in 1869 Pennsylvania and Illinois, and in 1871 Michigan established their own public boards and attempted to achieve the same ends.[4]

Taken together, then, public and private agencies reacted to the social crisis by attempting to modernize the treatment of the poor and dependent classes. They constituted a ruling class's war on poverty. They drew distinctions, as will be seen, between poverty (which they thought to be natural and unavoidable) and pauperism (which they considered wasteful dependency). They claimed to be working merely to eliminate the latter. But as social problems swelled out of proportion to their ability to manage, and as the individual's ability to control his destiny weakened under the pressure of the centralizing economy, this distinction became more fanciful than real. The reformers had discovered modern poverty, and in their efforts to contend with it they insisted on traditional moralistic labels.[5] Unlike Mr. Homos, these men and women assumed that poverty was a necessary goad to human achievement and character; thus, as they often quoted from the Bible, "The poor ye have always with you." But their industrial and urban world had made men, especially working men, *dependent* on forces beyond their control. As the visitor from Altruria would have seen it, all poor people were paupers to the system. Likewise, the reformers persisted in the emphasis on voluntary accommodation in community relations rather than on guaranteed public rights. So the onus of this social reform was assumed more by private agencies (sometimes forcing government cooperation) than by what we would call public assistance. If it was a war on poverty, it was fought by vigilantes rather than by a public militia. That distinction gave this struggle its peculiar moralistic and righteous character and justifies, it seems to me, this study's focus on those voluntary associations as they attempted to organize to assure tradition, community, and character against social disintegration.

When one gets into the thought of these reformers, he discovers that the cherished traditions were those of the idealized American town. The literature and propaganda of the reform echoed the Puritan fathers and the self-help ethic that all imagined had sustained the New England communities and transformed the wilderness. It was not merely a Protestant Ethic in the ordinary meaning of that term, but being generated by the Protestant establishment the reform vision had its parochial focus. The traditions that were to be protected in America, the special social feel of community, was Protestant after all. The Catholic church—the church of the urban population who were most the cause of alarm —seemed not as appalled by the sight of poverty, begging, and vagrancy as was the Protestant. And while Jewish philanthropy organized to meet the social crises of these years, its historical concept of charity and community was far more tolerant of poverty and dependency than were the reformers.[6] It was the traditional Protestant community that was thought to be in jeopardy, so it is little wonder that Protestants rallied to save it.

The social flux made some Protestants believe that their Christian obligation compelled them to make the church and the gospel relevant to the lives of the underprivileged, and they moved to support the Social Gospel.[7] Others, who tended to believe in the creative and redemptive possibilities among the poor, were drawn into the urban laboratories that the settlement movement tried to create.[8] Some felt that the real need was to find a better means to distribute the wealth of the nation's product, and they hoped for ways to achieve that without revolution. But those who were more conventional and conservative, and wanted to shirk radical possibilities, sought to improve character and to uplift the depressed through reforms such as the Charity Organization Movement. They were not profound thinkers, but perhaps because they were more conventional and less imaginative than the others, their work grafted itself more easily onto the social organism. They left important legacies. They contributed, as we shall see, to the professionalization of social work,[9] and they served as an essential link between private philanthropy and the present welfare system (which honors its parentage through shared assumptions).

In this study I have chosen only to look at one group of reformers in one city, Boston. I think that this narrow focus is justified because it heightens the sense of paradox in this effort to hold men to a tradition of individualism, and to contrive devices which would honor older community ties in an age marked by collectivism, change, and corporate power. The contrasts between imagination and reality, the contradictions resulting from collisions of idealized tradition with real circumstance, can best be viewed in the particular reform process.

Choosing a single city for the study of charity reform, one could do no better than Boston. It had achieved its urban maturity, with all the attendant problems, before the middle of the nineteenth century. Its solid citizens had for a long time a keen sense of a stake in community order; except for some southern cities, no other in America could boast such an old and stolid community. Under the pressure of social change, Bostonians had quite early found charity reform to be critical to the maintenance of social order.[10] And nowhere was that order more tenaciously defended by men and women who presumed to be the guardians of tradition. More than most cities in the United States, Boston had, by the end of the Civil War, an established reputation for social reform. It was itself, and was seen by others, to be a leader in social improvement—health, education, welfare. It had, through its history, contributed important leaders to national movements. And in charity reform, people like Robert Treat Paine, Zilpha Smith, and Annie Adams Fields, among the many, were constant support and direction to those in other cities, as well as to the National Conference on Charities and Corrections. People who had been trained in that city's agencies went on to serve Chicago, Philadelphia, New York, St. Louis, and San Francisco, carrying the gospel of charity reform and a syllabus of new techniques. While agencies in most cities designed their reforms to serve their own peculiarities, most would agree that Boston was a model of reform. It is not too much to say that Boston's experience was national in that it served the national movement by its example, leadership, and experimentation.

Mr. Homos would have found little to like in the charity reform movement. It was too protective of class and property interests, and, despite its Christian rhetoric, left Christ pretty much out of its judgments. The charity reformers were torn between their commitment to progress and their insistence on maintaining traditional values. At the heart of their concern was the social fragmentation caused by the imperatives of urbanization and industrialization. A small core of Anglo-Saxon Bostonians tried to hold the community together around old ideals, and their bond was charity. But the effort was as futile as the problem was paradoxical. Progress, the very essence of the middle-class faith, made forever impossible the return to the community of their dreams.

NOTES

1. Robert Bremner, *From the Depths: The Discovery of Poverty in the United States* (New York, 1956); Roy Lubove, *The Professional Altruist: The Emergence of Social Work as a Career, 1880–1930* (New York, 1969); Allen F. Davis, *Spearheads For Reform: The Social Settlements and the Progressive Movement, 1890–1914* (New York, 1967); Clarke A. Chambers, *Seedtime of Reform: American Social Service and Social Action, 1918–1933* (Ann Arbor, Mich., 1967), are the most notable.

2. Daniel M. Fox, *The Discovery of Abundance* (Ithaca, N.Y., 1967); Simon Patten, *The New Basis of Civilization* (New York, 1907–1921).

3. Charles D. Kellogg, "Charity Organization in the United States," in National Conference of Charities and Corrections, *Proceedings*, XX (1893), 52–93.

4. Robert W. Kelso, *The History of Public Poor Relief in Massachusetts, 1620–1920* (New York, 1921); Jeffrey R. Brackett, *Supervision and Education in Charity* (New York, 1903), Ch. 2.

5. Bremner, *From the Depths*, for America's discovery of poverty.

6. Barbara Miller Solomon, *Pioneers in Service* (Boston, 1956).

7. Henry F. May, *Protestant Churches in Industrial America* (New York, 1949).

8. Davis, *Spearheads For Reform.*

9. Frank J. Bruno, *Trends in Social Work, 1874–1956* (New York, 1957); Lubove, *The Professional Altruist*, takes up the results of reform.

10. *The Memorial History of Boston, 1630–1880*, ed. Justin Winsor (Boston, 1886) IV, gives an excellent survey of early charitable activity.

2

From Eschatology to Social Ethic

It is difficult to imagine Americans with deep social concern finding much satisfaction in 1895. The nation was still caught in the throes of one of its most severe depressions, human suffering in ghettoed cities screeched amidst the unbelievable affluence of the new urban rich, and the relations between management and labor in American industry seemed worse than they had ever been. Yet for those who believed that the primary task of humanitarianism was to insure the independent, moral character in the face of poverty and the industrial-urban onslaught, there appeared to be reason for celebration. The campaign by charity reformers to organize and propagate against easy public and private alms, street begging, vagrancy, and all other such symptoms of character disintegration could claim, by 1895, remarkable success. Both private and public agencies throughout the country had adopted and advanced reform precepts. Distinctions were being made everywhere between the worthy and unworthy poor, indoor and outdoor charity; welfare institutions were coming under severe criticism (with hardly a defender anywhere); cities were attempting to register and regulate all relief activity and to report the data from its records; the National Conference of Charities and Corrections was each year growing stronger and more influential among those who made decisions about public and private charity. Hardly a person in America who was knowledgeable about social problems and poverty was innocent of the doctrines of charity reformers. All of this was good news, indeed, to those who believed that America's greatest danger lay in possibly succumbing to sentiment and the needs of the poor without discrimination and, consequently, to the socialistic destruction of individualism and property.

Francis Greenwood Peabody, Plummer Professor of Christian Morals at Harvard University, was a man to find much to applaud in the state of charity reform. His own humanitarian credentials were unquestioned. A Unitarian minister, Peabody had for some years attracted divinity students and undergraduates at Harvard to courses in social ethics, where he attempted to explore the relevancy of Christian teachings and ethics to real social problems. Through his agency, many a young man found a new calling in social work with the poor. Flanked on the left by the more radical Social Gospel and Christian Socialism, Peabody was always ready to make distinctions which placed the onus of poverty on the character of the poor. Thus, thinking of the period just ended which had culminated in the maturity of charity reform, Peabody had reason to be pleased.[1]

Reflecting on the past, however, Peabody marked the "epoch of philanthropic renaissance" to have been fifty years in the past. The 1830s and 1840s in Boston were the decades when the first classical formulation of the problems of modern charity had been made in this country and the broad outlines of charity reform sketched. And he claimed that the two men most responsible for this early work were William Ellery Channing and Joseph Tuckerman.[2] The claim cannot be dismissed as parochial loyalty of one Unitarian for others. Channing's voice in religious and social reform is well known, Tuckerman was a classmate and a very close friend of Channing. After twenty-five years of ministering to a parish, he turned to the work of a city missionary among the Boston poor. He called this new service which he founded a Ministry-at-Large, and it remained part of the Unitarian program far after Tuckerman's death in 1840. Tuckerman expounded three principles of charity—the abolition of outdoor relief, the organization of the forces of charity, and personal visitation to the poor—forty years before they were generally applied by the charity organization societies. He anticipated what was to be called the science of charity by almost half a century.[3]

But the reforms that were urged by Tuckerman in the 1830s were not original with him. He acknowledged a debt to Thomas Chalmers, the Scottish common-sense theologian, who had transformed his own parish by strict adherence to principles of self-help. Chalmers had been rector of St. John's Parish in Glasgow from 1819 until he took a chair in philosophy at St. Andrew's College in 1823. As rector, he instituted reforms in poor relief which worked toward improved care at lower costs. His writings on the subject of his experiences influenced charity reformers in Britain and the United States throughout the remainder of the nineteenth century.

Thomas Chalmers had objected to the way the English Poor Laws had changed the management of charity in his Glasgow parish. The Scottish tradition of local autonomy had been changed so that contributions of the various parishes were collected into a general fund and distributed according to demand. After great insistence, Chalmers was able to get permission to control the funds of his parish without interference from the General Sessions; his own parishioners would not be allowed to receive outside alms, and St. John's

Parish would not be responsible for nonresidents. Chalmers divided his parish into small districts, each under the management of a deacon, who was responsible for visiting the poor within his ward and distributing the necessary alms. The sum regularly collected in the parish was all that the deacons had to work with. The experiment proved remarkably successful. The parish was able to get by on the eighty-pounds' contribution without calling on the Town Hospital. Indeed, in the second year of operation St. John's was able to remove all of its residents from town care and endow a parish school, paying the salaries of three teachers.[4]

Chalmers' experiment rested on three key convictions. First, he insisted on a distinction between pauperism and poverty; one was a state of unnecessary dependence, while the other was a matter of temporary misfortune. Chalmers further contended that legal or statutory relief was not only ineffectual, but it tended to pauperize since it removed the need for self-help. The third tenet followed. The relief-giving agent must deal with the smallest possible unit. The wards had to be small and the deacons had to have a few families that they knew intimately; self-help could thus be encouraged. The poor man naturally found relief, Chalmers held, first through his own effort, and then through his family, and then his neighbors. Relief came in a series of concentric circles, with the self at the center.[5]

Adhering to such principles, Chalmers achieved great economies while, at the same time, providing better than standard relief for the poor. Chalmers left Glasgow in 1823. The reform lasted until 1837, but without vigorous leadership St. John's reverted to the former program. But the experiment had been successful, and the lines of argument laid down. Chalmers' principles were to be referred to often in America before the turn of the century.[6]

It is not surprising that in the 1830s, when the reassessment of methods of poor relief was being urged on Bostonians, Dr. Joseph Tuckerman led the reform-minded to Thomas Chalmers' principles. Other American cities, notably New York, were attempting to systematize their charitable activities much in the same way as Boston in these years. In New York City, the efforts produced the Association for Improving the Condition of the Poor in 1843,[7] while Boston managed a major conference of charitable societies and established two major relief organizations attuned to the new spirit. Tuckerman had worked for several years to bring about a community-wide evaluation of its service to the poor before he succeeded, in February 1834, in getting delegates from the various benevolent societies to confer.

The delegates intended to "ascertain how far the various . . . Societies in this city can cooperate together . . . for a more systematic method of distributing charitable funds." Subsequently the committee avowed its interest in the "physical and moral wants of the Poor of this city." It found that while the societies devoted to helping the poor were numerous, "pauperism has increased to an extent which calls for the immediate and serious investigation" by those who feel an interest. The committee believed that numerous societies operating separately and independently were inadequate "to relieve the real and just wants of the poor" and were "highly injurious to society at large by encouraging extravagance, idleness, and vice." This committee, representing twelve Boston charitable societies, proposed an investigation and the publication of a report which would instruct interested persons in efficient means of charity.[8]

The problem in Boston, they thought, was easy enough to explain. Boston had always had a large number of benevolent societies, enough to care for the normal needs of the city as it had been. The societies always had insisted on autonomy, partly from pride in their purpose but also because of reluctance to "excite public observation." Each society, therefore, treated vice and fraud in its own way. When the population

was small, the report observed, this method was judicious;
"for it was desirable to ascertain how far public institutions
could resemble the quiet and secret almsgiving of individuals,
who are charged 'not to let their right hand know what their
left hand doeth.' " The committee noted that the benevolent
societies had increased in wealth and numbers as the city's
population had grown and that every "species of distress and
every class of subjects would seem to be provided for," but
"poverty has increased also, and to such an alarming extent as
to demand the careful and serious consideration of every
individual who has any regard for his own rights, or for the
welfare of the poor."[9]

Calls for charity had increased while "the amount of real
distress, excepting that which arises from vice, is not, in their
opinion, greater than it was many years since." More people
were totally dependent upon charity "and demand their
charity as a right"; more truly deserving got more than was
their need; more who deserve nothing "by artifice and decep-
tion get a good and entire support from charity." Observing
this corruption of a noble work, the committee confessed that
charity itself was largely responsible for its own deterioration,
for "not more than one half of what is given in charity goes
to the actual relief or prevention of real distress."[10]

The problem was one of inefficiency. While, for instance,
the organizations represented on the committee refused aid
without visiting the applicant, they did not share their intelligence; thus the visiting had limited use. "How can the members of a committee tell," they complained, "how many
societies and individuals have already assisted an applicant,
or how many have found out that he deserves no assistance
whatsoever?" They doubted that the applicant would confess.
He might receive aid from several societies, or he might have
been refused by many, and no other benefactor would be the
wiser. This lack of system and organization worked a hardship on the honest and moral poor, while the undeserving,

artful, and cunning were free to exploit all the charities of the city. The committee had no illusions. "One or two feet of wood once a month is to be sure not too much for a poor man," but when this was multiplied by ten or twelve different societies, it worked an inequity on the poor and a hardship on society. The report asserted that it was so easy to deceive societies and take aid from several of them that the poor often refused to accept even sufficient aid from one organization only.[11]

Reform, the committee found, was urgent; charitable people had to reassess their true responsibilities. If the object of charity was the raising of the poor to independence, was it not unwise, they asked, to give and encourage idleness, extravagance, and imposition? Sympathy could overcome reason. Is it possible "in our desire to gratify the benevolent feelings of our hearts, we are laying the foundation of a greater moral evil?" The almoner had a responsibility for the funds of the societies he represented. He could not treat even the smallest sums lightly. For, not only did it betray trust to give to the undeserving, but such gifts injured the recipient as well. By such kindness "we most assuredly are holding out strong inducements to the poor to beg and deceive, and are, in fact, giving them what they are often known to claim—a right to call upon us for a share of our bounty." The poor could not be blamed for taking advantage. The givers, alone were responsible.[12]

The great evil was the destruction of the character of the poor. While it was easy enough to accept gifts lightly given and to rely upon one's right to relief, the long-run effect was the enfeeblement of character by the weakening of one's independence. The committee saw two major objectives of reform. The first was to curtail imposition. The second was to adopt some means "by which the exact amount of charity given to each poor individual in the city shall be known by the Standing Committee of every Benevolent Society." The

need was clear; applicants must be investigated more carefully, and the societies had to cooperate more than had been
their habit.[13]

A plan was suggested. The city should be divided into
twelve districts, each with visitors from every society. Organized in district committees, these visitors could oversee their
area's poor relief and set up their own rules, "but in all cases,
*each delegate shall alone have the right to distribute the
funds of the Society to which he belongs.*" The societies could
continue their old forms, and changes were not meant to
"apply to those poor who are assisted in a private way, and
whose names, from motives of delicacy, it is desirable to con-
ceal." Thus, there was a reluctance to break habit or intrude
on the prerogatives of established societies. Otherwise, the
names of the district's poor would be gathered into a central
file and visitors could choose their cases. The applicant, then,
would know to whom he was to turn for assistance; he could
go nowhere else among private agencies. Delegates from each
district committee were to meet occasionally to share city-wide
intelligence. Thus they hoped to help the deserving and discover the frauds. The incorrigibles were to be referred to the
Overseers of the Poor.[14]

The advantages of such a reform were clear. The frauds
would be detected by the district organization. Those who
through reticence never received enough would be discovered
and aided. The former would be thus encouraged to exercise
economy, while the latter "would be able to thank God that
modesty and worth did not go unrewarded." The reform
would provide every poor family with a visitor, "fully ac-
quainted with its wants, well known and easily accessible
upon all occasions." These visitors were to be advisers and
friends to the poor, rather than almoners.[15]

Joseph Tuckerman, writing the first annual report of the
Association of Delegates from the Benevolent Societies of
Boston, was quick to acknowledge the Association's debt to

Thomas Chalmers. They had proceeded on Chalmers' assumption that alms were misgiven and abused, and they accepted his distinction between poverty and pauperism, contending also that the first aid was self-help.[16]

There were, of course, differences in emphasis. By the poor the Association meant those "who depend upon charity or alms for the means of subsistence." This dependence for the able-bodied was, of course, temporary. Pauperism, on the other hand, was "referable only to the poverty which is accompanied with abjectness and debasement." Chalmers had seen the debasement of the poor to be brought about by compulsory or legal assessment for poor relief which might be expected as a right. Tuckerman, writing for the Association, claimed that private agencies as well as public poor laws could pauperize. Benevolent societies, Tuckerman held, were known by the poor to be a ready source of relief. "Like the poor laws," he said, "they must and will operate as lures to applications for relief." Because they were impersonal, these societies even attracted people who would not appeal to a private benefactor. Tuckerman recognized, however, that American cities, unlike English, were not divided into autonomous parishes where the church had administrative control. Rather, Boston charities had to be city-wide in scope, and this necessitated an organization and cooperation among churches, benevolent individuals and societies to bring order to their work.[17]

The Association considered alms as relief doomed to fail; the low moral character of the poor necessitated the spur of discomfort. The Association reported individuals and heads of families "capable of labor, who will not themselves toil while they can live upon the toils of others." These people were lazy and indisposed to work. "They had rather beg than work; and as far as they can, they live, if not by beggary, upon alms." There were others who were never able to live within their incomes; "they might live in great comfort upon their earnings, if they would deny themselves what they cannot afford, and were willing to appear to be simply what they are. But they are more desirous to appear, than to be, what they are not." Such people depended upon alms because they were available. They would not be so dependent "if they felt a proper self-respect, and were under the guidance of a higher principle of right, and honor, and duty." Many, it was insisted, who suffer from occasional, "and even considerable," failures in employment might weather these difficulties if they anticipate bad times and show more frugality during favorable seasons. Almsgiving in such instances would become an encouragement to thriftlessness. Recognizing this human frailty, alms were a delicate tool for social amelioration. The single purpose of the Association was to guard against their abuse and misuse.[18]

The Association, through Joseph Tuckerman, articulated the principles which were to become the doctrine of the charity organization movement some thirty-five years later. They wanted to make clear that they did not think every applicant to be dishonest until he proved he was. They expected to make mistakes, but they wanted those errors in judgment to be a part of a record so that they would not be repeated. The Association thought its real value to be in providing communication and intelligence among its various members.[19] Among its assertions was the notion that laws against begging were not enough; benevolent societies and individuals had to make begging impossible. As a principle they insisted "*that individuals and families that ask for alms, are to be relieved only at their homes, and after a personal examination of each case; and that relief in cases, when given, is to be, not in money, but in the necessaries required in the case.*"[20] They insisted that alms should not interfere with the "*necessity of industry, forethought, and a proper self-denial.*" The dependent should not be allowed to "*live more comfortably without industry and economy than the humblest of the industrious and self-denying, who receives no alms.*"[21] And for the poor who were industrious, frugal, and self-respecting, "*with a preference of self-denial to dependence upon alms,*" the proper encouragement was not to be charity at all. Rather, what such men needed was sympathy and intelligent guidance, in short, a friend.[22] And, finally, the Association argued that no society should stand before the family and friends in support to the needy. The God-given obligations between parent and child should not be usurped by outsiders, regardless of good intentions.[23]

Despite their emphasis on rules and principles, the real object of this Association was to return charitable activity to personal and human interaction. Tuckerman, like Chalmers, objected not to alms per se, but to their formalization. Whether formalized through public law, established funds, or benevolent societies, there was the same destructive effect. Where the poor knew there was relief in government or in private agencies, they would expect it as a right and ignore their own obligation to self-help. The rich, on the other hand, would feel that their compulsory assessment or regular donation satisfied their obligation to the poor. To both Chalmers and Tuckerman, the duty of Christian charity required far more than the occasional or regular gift of money; it required in large measure a devotion of self to the service of the poor. The reemphasis of personal charity—where rich and poor could touch in sympathy—was to be achieved through the voluntary visitor. In addition, as one would expect, Joseph Tuckerman insisted that the church should be remembered as a place of charitable service.[24]

Tuckerman believed that the congregation should form the community through which true charity would be dispensed, and that the ultimate end of charity reform was to make alms the product of Christian and fraternal sympathy within the church itself.[25] Despite this emphasis, however, the lasting influence of Tuckerman and the Association was in their demand for city-wide organization, their criticism of alms as a means of social amelioration, and their insistence on visiting and investigating every applicant. When the demand for charity reform began to affect major cities in the late 1870s, it was these principles which were given new voice, and nothing much was said about Tuckerman's congregation. Boston's Associated Charities came close to achieving the city-wide organization of charities after its founding in 1879, a goal which evaded the grasp of the Benevolent Societies of Boston. A major cause of its frustration was that its member organizations[26] were of too limited interest to have incorporated the whole of its work. Two new charitable societies, however, took its principles as their guide. The Society for the Prevention of Pauperism and the Boston Provident Society were imbued with the spirit and intent of the Benevolent Societies of Boston.

The Society for the Prevention of Pauperism was started, in fact, by Joseph Tuckerman in 1835, and can be considered a continuation of the Association. The Society's concern was with men who were reduced to begging and relief because of an inability to find work. It established itself as an "intelligence" (employment) agency. It gave only jobs, neither money nor goods. As a free employment agency it considered itself a mediator between capital and labor; it encouraged employers to offer jobs as a kind of charity. Of course, it could not always find jobs for those who wanted to work. In such instances it would refer "worthy" cases to the proper relief agency. Free from the task of almsgiving, and instrumental in the encouragement of self-help, the Society could see itself as advancing the new ideas.[27]

The Boston Provident Association was established sixteen years after the Society for the Prevention of Pauperism. This Association intended to be a community-wide benevolent association ministering to the needs of all deserving poor, giving limited and temporary relief after an investigation. It divided the city into twelve districts (roughly corresponding to wards) and assigned several voluntary visitors to each. Its policy was never to give money but aid in kind, and never that to the inebriate. Contributors were given tickets to refer beggars to the Association for investigation and relief; all persons, however, were encouraged to refer beggars, because the hope was to remove them from the streets of Boston. As early as 1853 the Provident collected a "black record" of 201 names of impostors or persons not deserving relief. Considering itself a clearinghouse for the relief of Boston's poor, the Provident kept complete records and gave information about any applicant.[28]

From its establishment to 1879 the Provident wanted to build a city-wide organization to rationalize Boston's charities. In 1853 it attempted to merge with the Society for the Prevention of Pauperism, the Howard Benevolent Society, and the Society for the Employment of the Female Poor.[29] And in the following year it asserted that the increase of foreign poor necessitated the establishment of a central administrative agency; the Provident wanted "to become a kind of framework within which all the different charities of the city may act more intelligently and efficiently."[30] Failing in its first gestures for merger, the Provident suggested a single building where all the city's charitable societies might have offices.[31] Such a building, it was understood, would allow the exchange of information and facilitate the exposure of impostors. The Provident, however, found the other societies still too jealous of their autonomy. The committee on merger with the SPP reported "that the objects of the two Societies are distinct and not conflicting, and that a union, strictly so called, is not to be desired."[32] The idea of a charities building, however, seemed to satisfy everyone. The advantages seemed ample. Yet, nothing was done to further the building until 1863, when under the fresh inspiration for rationalization of welfare, occasioned by the establishment of the Massachusetts

Board of Charities, the Provident began to raise funds.[33] Charity Building on Chardon Street was completed in 1869 and realized a dream of Robert C. Winthrop, the Provident's president.

The building was not a satisfactory substitute for organization. The few societies that moved in were no more willing to cooperate under one roof than they had been under many. The Provident insisted there was still a need for unification. Of the sixty or seventy charitable institutions of the city, only twelve or thirteen, the Provident claimed, administered general relief, and Overseers of the Poor alone accomplished more than these. "It is evident," the Provident complained, "that these . . . associations . . . cannot accomplish the same amount of good that they might . . . under a central organization." Aside from duplication in administration, "the danger of imposition on the part of designing and deceitful applicants is immensely increased."[34] The Provident continued to express this idea with even greater urgency in the difficult early 1870s. But, as time went on, the Provident found that new little societies were formed to treat every special problem in some special way. Organization seemed to be a losing struggle, but the Provident battled continuously— even if alone among private agencies—down to the end of the eighth decade.[35]

Although these charitable societies, in their efforts at reform, were preoccupied with the nature of poverty and the conditions of the poor, they never suggested that there might be social or economic inequities that needed reform. Oddly, these men who were compelled to define the poor and calibrate qualities of impoverishment, who were convinced of the uniqueness of the lower classes, little anticipated or dreaded social unrest; classes in the European sense did not exist. These men and women were repulsed by the expected growth in the ranks of beggars and paupers. They knew, without argument, that each additional pauper was potentially vicious and criminal; men and women who lived off the alms had too little self-respect to be law-abiding. Yet, they called for little beyond a controlled benevolence. Only occasionally, and almost inadvertently, did the harsh light of social unrest pierce the haze of social theory.

When it did, however, it was subdued by faith in the poor's complacency. When Joseph Tuckerman, for instance, pointed out the frightening and threatening prospect of a continually enlarging pauper class, like those of London and Paris, born annually into degradation and crime where there was "little sympathy between the rich and the poor, but much contempt of the poor among the rich, and great exasperation, and equal hatred of the rich among the poor," there was only the feeblest hint of revolution in his language. Society was protected because the paupers and criminals were ignorant of their own power; they were disunited and the state and law were against them. What Tuckerman threatened, rather than revolution, was the necessity of a police state to control the depressed.[36]

Lacking either concern for fundamental social reform or anxiety about social upheaval, the charitable of Boston were content to find categories for the poor. The worthy poor—helpless by their youth or age, physical or mental disability—were those to whom society was always obliged. Worthy also were those who were temporarily embarrassed because of unemployment or business failure. But temporary is relative, and one might wonder how long an unemployed, able-bodied man might receive help without falling into the slough of dependence. The best proof of a man's worth was his assertion of self-respect through his reluctance to ask for aid. Ideally, it would seem, a man should resist alms to the last inch of his endurance; or, more precisely, until concern for his wife and children forced his humiliation. The unworthy poor, on the other hand, was a vague category which grouped together those who were too willingly and too long dependent on alms—criminals, tramps, beggars, vagrants—and those who demanded alms (or anything else they had not earned) as a right.

The failure of the poor was not their poverty but their poor characters. Thus, causes always remained with the poor themselves. "The main, if not the entire, cause of pauperism," insisted the SPP, "in a prosperous city like Boston, is *intemperance.*" And only five pages later it was argued: "Whatever tends to lessen the morals of a community tends to increase pauperism." In this instance the SPP criticized "sabbath-breaking boys," but also those who went to lectures on "Spiritualism, Mesmerism, Mormonism, and other *isms,*" for corroding morals. The poor must be encouraged to attend church that they might better sense their responsibilities to themselves and society.[37]

Despite good intentions it was difficult to visualize the poor in this way and still treat them like adults. In glaring contrast to the leaders of the social settlement movement (not to begin until the 1890s),[38] charity reformers never suggested that the poor might have special insight into their own problems; they were the last to be consulted about their interest. "Most of them are seeking an easier way of getting a living, and few are inclined to pursue the calling to which they were educated. If mechanics, laborers, or farm-hands, they want to get into a store or do some light work; if servants for 'Family's work,' they want situations as nursery-maids, chamber-maids, or seamstresses." Thus, the poor had to be guided, told, scolded, cajoled, pushed and even punished. Reverend Rufus W. Clark expressed this sense of paternity. "When it is borne in mind how much care is exercised that every person who goes from our offices shall be sent only to respectable employments and with respectable persons, where they shall be as safe as under a parent's roof, it will be seen that a great amount of good is effected by the Society." It would appear that the stewardship of the rich meant a kind of parenthood to the poor.[39]

Such a view of the poor exposed an assumption of a simple society. For always lurking behind the arguments, the principles and the rules, was the conception of a city that was smaller, more homogeneous, with more easy and natural relations between rich and poor than was the reality of the speaker's Boston. Whatever the facts, the remembered city was small, rich and poor were familiar to one another, and help was given on the basis of known character. Real or unreal, that past city always served as both a wistful recollection and a stern measure for present conduct. In those happier days "pauperism was a thing determinable in nature and quantity." The population was homogeneous. "The poor were personally subjects of knowledge and cognizance to the more favored classes. Every man was known by his neighbor. . . . Improvidence, vice, and recklessness . . . existed then, it is true, as now." Intemperance was no stranger to the city. But people were more subject to the censure of public opinion. "Few were . . . indifferent to the shame and reproach of a total forfeiture of the goodwill, respect, and confidence of the better classes of the society; for, in short, none was overlooked, nor could escape in the crowd."[40]

But even as early as 1858 the charitable were conscious that, whatever the truth of their recollections, Boston had changed beyond any resemblance to this self-regulating paradise. Complaints were already voiced, in this antebellum year, of the "influx of foreign pauperism, ready-made and hatched abroad." These strangers helped to swell the size of the city's poor which was already increased by "our native poor, who remove to Boston from the country for the purpose of getting aid from the charitable institutions of the city. They find help more readily than at home, where they are better known." Whatever was wrong could be left at the door of new people because of failure of traditional control.[41] The men and women who worked in charitable societies wanted to reestablish that social control. Thus, the Provident could justify itself in 1879 as an agency which was replacing the personal

investigation of the older, simpler community: "to practice
the virtue of charity to the poor, in a great city, requires the
aid of benevolent corporations." And the "scientific spirit of
this age in manifested in the management of charities." The
whole matter of charity had become too complex for the
benevolent individual.[42]

The magnitude of the problem, however, did not affect
the charitable's view of the poor; no matter how large the
city or how heterogeneous, the poor were still merely worthy
or unworthy. Seldom was this bifurcation disrupted by concerns for social justice or equitable distribution; nor did
anxiety over social unrest disturb the neat division. Necessarily, adequacy of relief was never at issue. If anything, the
community thought itself too generous. Any offering, small
or large, was applauded for its virtue. The decent poor, of
course, would appreciate the smallest gesture, which was too
generous for those who would demand more. When ladies of
Hollis Chapel began the Flower Mission in 1869, they did not
question that flowers would benefit those in hospitals, poor
houses, slums, and schools. As one observer reported:

> As soon as the first flower was handed out the news spread like
> wild-fire, and the children would come in crowds from garret and
> cellar for the prizes, while men, rough laborers, would stop &
> beg,—more humbly than the children,—for "just one flower,
> Miss."[43]

Francis Peabody was justified in memorializing William
Ellery Channing and especially Joseph Tuckerman as the
progenitors of the modern philanthropic movement. Yet,
while Peabody was pleased to celebrate the fathers of his age,
he was nevertheless aware that some quality of spirit had gone
out of the enterprise since their time. The generational difference had to do with his contemporaries' almost total preoccupation with social (as opposed to religious) concerns.
"The absorbing interest in philanthropy," Peabody feared,
"may involve a certain contempt for that which is not im-

mediately practical." The relevancy of churches was challenged so that they were becoming mere organizations of
social reform. "We are inclined to beat our spears of theological conflict into pruning hooks of social redemption. Thus
the age of works succeeds the age of faith."[44] Channing and
Tuckerman, after all, considered their primary obligation to
be the souls of men and the soul (there is no better word) of
the community; they were evangelists. As Robert Bremner
makes clear, the first concern of these men was to bring
religious comforts to the unchurched poor.[45] By the end of
the century, however, these were no longer the priorities of
even churchmen working with the poor. This spiritual gap
between the generations can best be illustrated by comparing
the social attitudes of William Ellery Channing and one of
his intellectual heirs, Edward Everett Hale.

In 1841, William Ellery Channing took the occasion of a
eulogy for Joseph Tuckerman to spell out his thoughts on the
problems of the contemporary city and the Christian obligation of one citizen for his brother. It was a remarkable discourse—surveying urban ills much like our own, but wholly
within the context of a primary Christian ethic.[46]

Because of its dynamics and tumult, Channing looked to
the city to test the Christian quality of people. The religious
demands were for harmony, equality, and community, while
the imperatives of business worked toward competition, social
differentiation, and fragmentation. A true Christian spirit was
the only solution to this paradox. Moral obligation, human
sympathy, and, above all, charity were the ligaments holding
the city in delicate tension, allowing the greatest material
progress under the most perfect moral restraint.

Channing understood it was God's intention that cities
work toward human interdependence. Multiplicity of human
wants bound men together. They were to understand one
another's perils and sufferings and "act perpetually on one
another for good." God, reasoned Channing, intended men

to have a social destination. Men are city-bound that they may propose a "common weal"; that they "seek each other's highest good."

Men were bound, according to Channing, to absolute standards of justice. The human condition was not to be left to impersonal natural laws, free to rise or fall in a laissez-faire society. A Christian determinant must insure fair distribution of wealth so that the "means of comfort and improvement are liberally diffused." But even with the most perfect justice, he was willing to admit, some would be poor. So there was religion's surest demand: "to rescue them from the degrading influence of poverty, to give them generous sentiments and hopes, to exalt them from animals to men, into Christians, into children of God." The truly happy city honored human nature. The saddest thing about contemporary cities, he exclaimed, was their fragmenting because of their growth. In most large cities there were two societies, knowing little of one another, worlds apart. In London, Channing observed, one could plunge from the heights of affluence to the depths of want merely by crossing three streets. This estrangement of man from man and class from class was, to Channing, the measure of social imperfection and man's real challenge.

It was the challenge of his Bostonians; it was evil for men to grow up and die without knowing how the multitude lived. He urged his readers into the damp cellars "where childhood and old age spend day and night, winter and summer." They should scale to the upper room "which contains within its narrow and naked walls, not one but two and even three families." They should go beyond seeing the poor in the streets; they should meet them in their cheerless homes. The Christian had to be his brother's keeper, but not alone through charity—spiritual uplift was part of the social bargain. The only way that the community could be held together, despite its growth, was by concentrating on the essentials: man, himself, and his moral condition.

Crime prevention was one means by which all humanity could be enhanced. Channing, however, advocated a program not to protect the victims of crime but to save the potential criminal. "Society ought not to breed Monsters in its bosom." If the community encouraged vice "by its selfishness and luxury, its worship of wealth, its scorn of human nature, then it must suffer, and deserves to suffer, from crime." By such a measure, Channing held Bostonians responsible for much of the crime and misery around them. Because something could be done, "much of the guilt and misery around us, must be imputed to ourselves." Children are abandoned to ignorance. Nothing is done to break the "fatal inheritance" of beggary. Human sympathy, Christian sympathy, were it to penetrate the dwellings of the ignorant, poor, and suffering, were its voice lifted up to encourage, guide, and console, and its arms stretched out to sustain, what a new world would it call into being!"

Channing would not be put off by stock arguments. To those who wished to excuse themselves from social duty because they took care of themselves and their families, Channing insisted that the private circle could not remain pure amidst general impurity. "If any member of the social body suffer, all must suffer with it. This is God's ordination and his merciful ordination." To those who were apathetic, cynical, or stoical—claiming that society could not be improved —Channing's was a voice of confidence and progressivism. The world, civilization, had improved, he claimed, and Christianity had been a catalyst.

Progress, however, could intensify problems; it was not an unmixed blessing. The city was growing. Most people, Channing claimed, were pleased with the prospect and anxious to stimulate growth and the prosperity that would go with it. But he warned them about the problems of growth; he pointed to other cities. Often they have drawn the abandoned, have bred a "horde of ignorant, profligate, criminal poor."

And the cities have been deformed by the horrible contrast between luxury and proverty. He was not against growth. But may "God withhold prosperity, unless it is to be inspired, hallowed, ennobled by public spirit, by institutions for higher education, and by increasing concern of the enlightened and opulent, for the ignorant and poor." Thus, in Channing's ideal city, property, privacy, and progress were secondary to humane and spiritual ends. This imperative for Christian community obligation was not mere language. The Ministry-at-Large in Boston was an agency which he supported that attempted to put these ideals into practice.

In his observations about the growth of the city, William Ellery Channing had been a true prophet. In the fifty years that followed his discourse, Boston burst with new people. The Irish, already coming in Channing's time, came in even greater numbers for a few years, then slacked off. The older Jewish population from western Europe was submerged by Jewish refugees from the pogroms of eastern Europe. And there were the Italians. The historic North End, the newer South End, and the West End (the back side of Beacon Hill) were given over to strange people and new accents. The older Bostonians—those who could—retreated out of town, to the newly filled Back Bay, or they clung to their side of Beacon Hill. Those who could not move often shriveled in their single rooms, their lodging houses—strangers in their own city. Losing all else, they fondled nativity, their last possession. The city grew with Americans too. New England agriculture could no longer hold onto its labor. Farm laborers, the sons and daughters of farmers, and even the farmers themselves and their families moved to Boston. By the last decade of the nineteenth century, Boston could boast all of the problems of a full-fledged city. There were beggars, vagrants, itinerants, and slums. Industry had brought a new prosperity, but prosperity emphasized class distinctions. And with it all, as Channing predicted, there was vice.[47]

The "Jesus" of Edward Everett Hale, however, saw few problems in Boston which were not in proper hands and well on the way to solution. *If Jesus Came to Boston* was Hale's answer to W. T. Stead's *If Christ Came to Chicago.* Hale did not wish to abate the force of Stead's warning that "we are all going to hell remarkably fast" since Christ's plan had been ignored. Neither did he wish to contrast Boston and Chicago, which he considered "curiously alike in many important regards." Hale was merely more sanguine; he wanted to show a happier side. After all, hells, slums, dives, adultery, gambling, opium, and murder exist everywhere. "I could show it all to him here, as I could have showed it to him in Jerusalem or Tiberias, or as they can in Chicago now," Hale had his narrator say. But, he claimed, there were other things, good things, which could be shown to Jesus in Boston "which I could not have shown him in Jerusalem or Nazareth or Bethlehem."[48]

Dr. Hale's little book is a narration by "Dr. Primrose" of his adventures with a stranger—perhaps Jesus—touring Boston in search of relatives. Because these relatives were poor, and possibly disreputable, the two men were taken to all of the major social welfare agencies in the city. They went to the Traveller's Aid. The Associated Charities maintained a card file of applicants for relief to all agencies which they used. They observed how the "margin" was handled by the Overseers of the Poor, who saw that "nobody is to starve while the Commonwealth has a penny left." It was explained to them that it was "wholly impossible" to give money to anyone in need; "it might go for whiskey. The city prefers to give the food itself, which is to go into the mouth of the hungry." They visited the Provident Association, which gave food, clothes, and fuel to the poor. And they called on the Industrial Aid Society, which tried to find jobs for the unemployed. The lost relatives were not found, but "Dr. Primrose" received a message the next morning from the stranger: "*I*

*have gone to Chicago. I find I have other sheep there. What
you in Boston have been doing to the least of these my
brethren and sisters, you have done it unto me.*"[49]

Whether or not Jesus would have been pleased with
Boston's care of the "least of these," Edward Everett Hale
was. Hale applauded the fact that there was a private society
to care for almost every kind of need, and public support for
the totally dependent who met legal standards. These agencies
knew each other's work, if not through their own intelligence,
then through the facilities of the Associated Charities. Things
ran smoothly. There were efficient professional people ready
to help at every turn. Charity and social welfare had been
worked into a science.

It is precisely this scientific certainty that distinguishes the
spirit of Hale's philanthropy from Channing's. One could
catalog their general points of view on charity and find them
almost identical in stated principles. Yet one distinction made
all the difference. Channing conceived of a community bound
by love of God for man, man for man, and a belief in human
dignity over property—a *true* philanthropy. Channing's citizen had to be kept cognizant of his Christian duty to his
fellow man. There could never be certainty. Hale, on the
other hand, saw a community of societies, run by experts,
which anticipated every legitimate need, and were run on
scientific principles. From a strictly religious point of view,
setting aside for the moment social welfare concerns, the most
notable thing about Dr. Hale's little book is the absence of a
minister to the poor. How different from Joseph Tuckerman!

Unlike Channing, Hale could not divorce material and
social progress from moral progress. And, according to Hale,
progress was everywhere to be seen. One could measure the
gradual movement of the world from "darkness, ignorance,
and suffering toward light, knowledge and happiness" by
comparing historical periods.[50] Although there was evidence
of sin and crime in the world—"it is impossible to exaggerate

the blackness of vice, or to paint sin in worse colors than it deserves"—men were not to be misled when a great artist succeeded in describing "a single crime," or portraying "the horror of sin in a single instance." Men must be wary of despair in the short view. The single instance did not prove that the world was running backward. "This would be really to say that there is no God ruling the world." The "great orb of history" must be viewed that one might estimate the progress of man and the imminence of the coming of the Kingdom of God.

And, for Hale, the facts and history were on God's side. One could look around and see. There were more good people in the world than bad people, more prosperous in America than poor. "The Christian church had not been mistaken in saying, for nineteen hundred years, that the Kingdom of God is coming." Indeed, Hale could see that the great day was already becoming, as evidenced in the number of communities in the United States that knew little of crime and nothing of pauperism.[51]

Much of Hale's mature work celebrated this coming of God's Kingdom. Aside from his pastoral labor, Hale edited two magazines. The short-lived *Old and New* announced itself as bringing to the service of the new and progressive that which was valuable from the old and traditional. His later effort, *Lend A Hand,* was from the first a semiofficial organ of the Charity Organization Movement. As such, this magazine turned over its pages to professional charity workers and charity reformers. But even here was the subtitle "A Record of Progress."[52]

Hale would not deny that problems existed. Of course, the very growth of cities caused social problems. But solutions merely awaited social awareness. Tenement conditions could be improved; enlightened citizens could make loans available to tenement dwellers for suburban housing developments.[53] The loneliness, isolation, and impersonality of the city could be reduced; a systematic program of voluntary visitors to the poor would bind all together.[54] Urban congestion could be eased; those who could afford it should begin a "return wave" to the country, to make a life, if not a living, on the farm.[55] Of course, industrial growth and capitalism had peculiar problems. But unemployment was largely a matter of geography. There were always jobs; the problem was merely to get available labor to available jobs. Low and unsteady wages were a problem of poor planning. Employers should plan so that men were hired throughout the year; thus seasonal gluts would not occur to affect the market.[56] In a capitalistic, competitive society there were industrial disputes; could there not be a High Court of America which would arbitrate?[57] And, at last, in those unproductive years, when the aged are dependent on their families or the community, could not there be an insurance system which would provide an adequate pension?[58] There were problems enough; Hale never claimed that the Kingdom of God had arrived. But all the problems were manageable. And, significantly, Hale always assumed that there was no real conflict between man's interest and God's purpose. Rational men operating in their own interest, once they saw the whole problem, would effect the Christian end.

Hale was intrigued with planning some organization or system which could work for the efficient elimination of social problems. His strong utopian inclination seemed to anticipate the Kingdom of God on earth. His model was always the ideal New England town of an imagined earlier day.[59] He imagined that city wards might serve the same end, if a kind of social minister were put in charge.[60] He naturally found utopian schemes and literature congenial to his mind. He found *Looking Backward* very suggestive.[61] He even wrote his own novels, spinning out his utopian notions. *How They Lived in Vineland* and *How They Lived in Naquadavick* were only less ambitious than *How They Lived in Hampton, A Study in Practical Christianity*. This last, his most elaborate, told how a wool manufacturing town was turned into a profit-sharing, cooperative commonwealth. The evidence around him of company towns, such as Pullman, Illinois, convinced Hale that the schemes were not mere dream stuff.[62]

Measured by national impact and by Edward Everett Hale, Jr.'s testimony, the Ten Times One is Ten Program was the most important of all of Hale's utopian schemes.[63]

The idea started from a piece of Hale's fiction about a man named Harry Wadsworth. Harry had died, and ten of his mourners at the railroad station waiting to depart from the funeral services began to talk about what Harry had been to them. It seems that Harry Wadsworth, an extremely good man, had done something requiring great self-sacrifice and courage for each of these people. This one man had improved the lives of at least ten others. What a powerful force for Good! This was too important a truth to ignore and forget. They resolved that each would try to be a Harry Wadsworth to ten others. This would be evidence of a lesson well learned. But more, the dynamism of the goodness thus released would be a living monument to their friend. According to the story, they did that; they formed the culture that grew other tens, which grew others, and the exponential increase soon covered the earth with people who wanted to be of service and to do good.[64]

The simplicity, the common sense, of the idea was its greatest force. Who had not thought, at one time or another, that if everybody did good to his neighbor, if everybody truly loved man, the whole world would be a world of good and love? Here was that idea in a system. One did not have to commit himself to a great, complex program of reform or marshal humanity under any specific banner. One merely had to be of service—to do good. It was easy enough, and one could see it grow.

Hale devoted several pages of *Lend A Hand* to the Ten

Times One clubs which began to spring up all over the country. Of course Harvard had a club; Wellesley had one too. Clubs started all over the East, and there were reports of "tens" in Michigan and even in Oakland, California. They adopted the motto: "Look up and not Down. Look Forward and not back. Look out and not in. And Lend a Hand." The columns in the magazine were devoted to reports of the clubs, what they did, how they found new and imaginative ways of doing good; and they asked help from others. Thus the magazine kept the clubs informed of each other's activities and existence. With the observable, rapid increase in number of these clubs, it was easy to suppose that in time the world, or at least a large portion of it, would be served by Ten Times One clubs.[65]

The significance of these clubs, for our purpose, is not their faddish popularity—spreading through the country, to die out in a few years. Rather, we should note that Edward Everett Hale considered the conception and the work he did to promote them the most important he had done. When one considers the plan of these clubs, along with Hale's other utopian schemes—where man, because of some innate sense of public good, mitigates his own selfish interest for the recognized community interest—one gains sharp insight into the religious thinking of Hale.

The absence of crisis in the thinking of Hale is what distinguishes him most sharply from his liberal predecessors. Both Hale and Channing saw the divinity of the human soul. Channing, however, saw an imperfect man in need of salvation—a word little used by Hale. Both Channing and Hale accepted a notion of progress. Channing, however, separated material progress from morality, and he cautioned that men must struggle to maintain their humanity in a world of affluence; Hale's world grew better by God's design, better morally as well as materially. Channing challenged men to accept the divinity that was rightfully theirs. Hale, on the other hand, urged men to lend a hand in speeding the promised coming.

The quality and spirit that Francis Peabody noticed had gone out of the philanthropic enterprise from Channing's time to his own may be defined by this distinction between Channing and Hale. What had been formerly doubt and imperative had become certainty and automatic—evolutionary and progressive. An earlier concept which saw social obligation as the means of civic redemption had become emasculated by the optimistic sense of the necessary coming of the Kingdom of God. Channing's religion was still that of personal and community salvation; there was always implied a final judgment. Hale's religion, on the other hand, reflected his times and was a social ethic.

It was precisely the social ethic that Edward Everett Hale represented that troubled Francis G. Peabody with the state of the church in philanthropy at the close of the century. As he put it, instead "of the study of the Hebrew prophets, we have the study of the prophets of socialism. Instead of salvation by Christ, people begin to look for salvation by legislation and hygiene."[66] While the immediate targets of Peabody's barbs were the Social Gospelers and the Christian Socialists, the phenomenon was general and infected, alike, conservative and liberal churchmen who wished to remain relevant to their times. The tendencies that Hale epitomizes were for churches to find their justification in the social environment, often at the expense of religious content.[67] Churches experienced this shift without conscious intent. The need to make adjustments to changing conditions forced many to "socialize" their religious effort. Charities, which were always the social arm of the church, were the first sign of this adaptation. Before mid-century, church-inspired charities worked for spiritual renovation; but by the century's end, religious purpose and content were scarcely apparent.

The pressure for change worked in two directions. The

churches tried with increasing diversity of program to satisfy community needs, and changes in the character of the community forced the churches to diversify. This was especially urgent as the new settlement houses proved more successful in reaching the unchurched poor. The experience of the Boston Port and Seamen's Aid Society provides an excellent illustration. Located in the North End, this society was forced to change because the North End changed. The fact of new people, alien to Protestantism, and the fact of a declining American merchant marine could not be ignored if the message was to remain vital.[68]

A few members of the Methodist Episcopal church had organized the Boston Port Society in 1829. Reverend Edward Thompson Taylor (Father Taylor), formerly a common sailor and a privateer in 1812, was hired to minister to sailors in the North End. The Port Society's major activity during the early years was to provide Protestant, nonsectarian services for sailors in their church in North Square. The Seamen's Aid Society, on the other hand, was founded in 1833 by a committee of women to assist Father Taylor's wife. This society of women opened a clothing store which gave employment to sailors' wives. In 1846 they opened the Mariner's Home, which competed with the lodging and rooming houses that exploited seamen.[69]

Little of material substance was given by either of these Societies. The sailors were expected to pay for their lodgings and supplies at the Mariner's Home. The Bethel, of course, merely served the sailor's spiritual wants. There was, however, provision for the needy. Sailors who were down and out were advanced the cost of their lodgings and outfit. If a man dissipated himself and his money in the brothels, gambling houses, or saloons, he could hope that the Seamen's Aid Society would lend him the necessary funds to make him shipshape. The Society merely advanced the cost, however; it expected to be repaid, and most often it was.[70]

In the early years, the Seamen's Bethel dominated the operation. Father Taylor was a fiery and effective preacher. His reputation had gone with his sailors throughout the world. Sailors who were strange to Boston's port knew of the Bethel flag and Father Taylor; they were prepared to expect the crowds that overflowed the church into North Square. Father Taylor's voice carried the even greater distance to the other side of Boston and stirred the lives and spirits of the respectable.[71] During his life the Port Society and its church were in their glory. The chapel was never large enough to hold the multitudes. The wealthy of Boston were convinced of a need to give, and they saw their efforts affecting large numbers.[72]

In 1871, after a long illness, Father Taylor died. Apparently, a great deal had depended on his dynamism, because the Seamen's Bethel began to lose its following as Father Taylor's illness forced him from the center of its activities. In the later 1860s a constantly changing clergy tried, through the annual reports, to explain the steady drop in attendance. Each justified his own work by quality—the actual conversion —rather than by the numbers in the pews. But no insistence on undiluted religious service could reverse the general decline in the congregation. Of course the old lures—brothels, gambling, and drink—served as a convenient explanation. However it was to be explained, the fact of falling attendance had to be faced. By 1884 the chapel that had been too small for the worshipers had become too large to justify maintenance. The church was given up in that year, and the Seamen's Bethel was moved into the Mariner's Home.[73] During the years of decline insecure ministers tried to prove their professional adequacy by the publication of testimonials.

After all, it was the human soul that mattered. So they would find a mate of a vessel who would testify: "I used to think I couldn't get along on shipboard, without swearing at the men and knocking them about; but since I came here and got converted, I have learned better, and get along much easier." Page upon page of such devotion would be printed, a quaint religion in metaphors of the sea:

> Another of equal interest was the case of a captain, whose mind being greatly disturbed, he rose, and, in tones of anguish, said: *"I have lost my reckoning*—am in the fog, and want light—will you help me?" We presented his case to the kindly notice of Him. . . . He arose, and said: "I have a little light, but it shines dimly; I am not satisfied." We encouraged him. " 'Tis increasing," said he; "I shall receive it"—and he did, and was soon rejoicing, with a heart overflowing with gratitude to God for his great salvation.[74]

So the quality was there; there was evidence enough. But the anguish of inadequacy plagued them. They seemed always to suspect that Father Taylor could have filled the house.

Doubtless Father Taylor had been a powerful preacher. But even he could not have been unaffected by changes which were occurring in the North End. There was, during these years, a decline in the number of American sailors entering into the Boston port. The North End, itself, had become by 1900 predominantly Italian and Jewish. The Protestant population had begun to decline in the years before Father Taylor's death.[75]

The Society had actually adjusted to these changes without much reassessment of its purposes. It began to use *colporteurs* who could speak languages other than English, mainly Scandinavian and Italian. They helped sailors sent from the British and Danish consuls. They turned their attention, more and more, to children and families of sailors, and also other children in the neighborhood. The reports began to announce lectures; the popular ones were on travel. Once the lectures were established in the program, they purchased a stereopticon to illustrate them. By the end of the century the activity of the Boston Port and Seamen's Aid Society had become quite diversified. Yet there never seemed to be a conscious effort in that direction.

By 1901 the Society appeared greatly changed in tone and purpose. In that year the minister applauded the entertainments and illustrated lectures that had been part of the program for several years. "Not that we ought to subordinate the religious element in our work," but men who follow the sea had no place for recreation outside of the Bethel, except for places "degrading in their influences." Indeed, he thought, the program should be enlarged; more should be offered. "What I should like to see . . . is a large building fitted much like any Y.M.C.A. . . . but with some additional features, such as a billiard room and lunch room, with a coffee-bar where at cost hot coffee and all temperance drinks could be obtained . . . with an interesting entertainment almost every evening, where new acquaintances could be formed."[76] Without any theory or planning the Boston Port and Seamen's Aid Society, under the pressure of changing times and environment, began to turn its attention to the more secular, the more social interests of its charges.

Nor was the Boston Port and Seamen's Aid Society an isolated case. Almost every Protestant church in Boston that worked directly with the poor experienced similar changes during the last three decades of the nineteenth century. Indeed, even Joseph Tuckerman's Ministry-at-Large followed the trend.

Originally, the Ministry-at-Large was intended to be a foundation of religious benevolence. As pastor, the minister made his way into the homes of the poor to raise the spirits of the destitute, to win the infidel and the skeptic back to the church, to save children from immoral influence, to give spiritual comfort to the aged and to find those in the community who would help reduce their physical discomfort, to find succor for the sick, cure the "disease" and "destroy the evil of Intemperance." But this was not all. The minister-at-

large was preacher as well as pastor. Through the chapel
he was to bring the poor together into one family. The poor,
like the rich, had their estrangements and enmities. And, like
the rich, they needed "to be humbled in the sense of their
common guilt, and be reconciled to each other, as they desire
and hope to be reconciled unto God." Taken together, the
pastoral ministry and the chapel attempted to serve the
spiritual needs of the poor (and to give the rich an opportunity to serve); nonreligious, physical relief was given to
achieve these ends.[77]

The Benevolent Fraternity of Churches, the heir to the
Ministry-at-Large, by the end of the nineteenth century supported five chapels throughout Boston. Cyrus A. Bartol and
the other Unitarian ministers of his time would have hardly
recognized them, however. Immigration which changed the
community population from predominantly Protestant to
Catholic and Jewish, cultural changes which caused the diminution of the social role of the clergy, social and economic
changes which began to dominate social reform all converged
to make new emphases and new demands on community
churches that wanted to remain vital. Nonreligious services
had already dominated the activities of these free chapels.
The North End Union, for example, boasted a gymnasium
and classes in dressmaking, plumbing, and printing; it had
playrooms, public baths, reading rooms, illustrated lectures,
stamp-savings plans, and monthly socials.[78]

All of these chapels had similar activities; some, however,
specialized. Henry Morgan, a licensed Methodist preacher
and the founder of Morgan Chapel, left his establishment, on
his death in 1884, to the Benevolent Fraternity of Churches.
The Chapel continued Morgan's interest of rehabilitating the
poor by teaching them trades. In 1885 Reverend E. J. Helms
began to shape its activities along the present-day lines of the
Morgan Memorial (Goodwill Industries): "The man who had
no trade sawed wood for the widow who had no fire; while

the widow made and repaired in turn the garments for others in need of them." The Chapel became a clearinghouse for the products of such labor. "A certain portion of the Chapel basement has at times looked like a hospital for old furniture."[79] Or, in the summer months the Bulfinch Place Church operated playrooms to keep the poor children off the streets. "The object of our playroom was not simply to give them a happy time, but by kindergarten songs and games and occupations to continue the elevating and civilizing influence of their school training, so that the summer months might not be wholly demoralizing."[80] One contemporary noted that the Parker Memorial had become a very institutional agency. It had originally intended "to be a Unitarian church, and still has religious services on Sundays. These, and the lectures and discussions on popular topics which occur on week-day evenings, appeal to the rather well-to-do people who live in the immediate neighborhood." But the more direct work of the Chapel was with the tenement dwellers who lived nearby. "The constituency of the clubs and classes is largely Jewish, though more children of American parents come here than to other social centres in these parts."[81]

Examples seem endless. Almost every church located in the North, South, and West Ends added programs to attract the poor by satisfying nonreligious needs.[82] On the one extreme, the Episcopal St. Stephen's maintained a coal and wood yard, giving work to men who wished to reform. This church catered to the laboring classes, although it boasted a congregation of both Back Bay and North End residents. St. Stephen's attempted, first, to satisfy spiritual needs; only secondarily did it try to meet the social demands of its constituents. In contrast, the Berkeley Temple regarded the reading rooms, entertainments, employment bureau, and classes as a means by which men might be brought within the hearing of the message. Like the Berkeley Temple, the Everyday Church used its recreation rooms, low-cost lunch counter, kindergarten, stamp savings bank, classes in music, sewing, and cooking, and university extension lectures as means to bring men into the Christian life. "Failing in this, it would believe that it was not fulfilling its real mission." Yet these churches, although differing in emphasis, still retained some part of their religious purpose. At the other extreme, however, the nonreligious activities of places like the Parker Memorial could so dominate the program that the chapel became an "institutional agency."[83]

Under the pressures of social change, the churches had to adapt themselves as well. If nothing else, the cultural heterogeneity of the urban poor made particular religious messages irrelevant. In the last decade of the century, the new social settlement challenged and led the city churches into diversified social service. The settlement workers were predisposed to honor the culture and religion of the people, presuming them to be means to community identification.[84] Protestant churchmen who wanted to be effective among the urban poor had little choice but to do the same. In the theory or the practice of religion, whichever is considered, the churchmen's focus was turned outward to the city. What had been salvation became social improvement or uplift. Where disagreement arose among the clergy, it tended to be about methods and principles of social service, not theology.

By the end of the nineteenth century, the Boston Protestant community had breathed a congenial air which diminished doctrinal disputation. This general good feeling went beyond the bounds of liberal Protestantism and was announced by the active laymen as well as the clergy. After affirming his belief in Christ, the president of the Boston Provident Association and a long-time Episcopalian vestryman, announced his creed, iterating the humanitarian assumption of Channing within the framework of the progressive evolution of Hale. Charles R. Codman asserted his belief that the great changes in history and the "vast material progress of mankind in these latter days are all a part of the great dispensation of that spirit who Christ told us would lead us into all truth." He noted that the old beliefs and theological formulas were being revised and renewed "and made spiritual in these days." Rigid definitions about "faith & works necessary for salvation—all of these things are giving away, and yet I believe there was never more real christianity than now." The progress was to continue, and "sooner or later, & by methods of which we . . . do not dream the Kingdom of the world will become the Kingdom of the Lord."[85]

Where progress trumpeted the inevitable Kingdom, preoccupation with the souls of the poor became less. Religious leaders turned their attention more and more to social adjustment—to make the community more like the imagined Kingdom. And the churches themselves, where they met the poor, exerted greater energy in nonreligious programs to attract and aid the poor. These two tendencies—both independent responses to changing urban conditions—were mutually reinforcing. A church that denigrated internal, personal revolution found it easier to occupy itself with secular, social reform activities; a church which occupied itself with a social program would find personal salvation irrelevant.

Where the spirit and program of Protestant churches became more secular, those charities which had been affected by the church shifted their ground as well. The activities began to have less than a purely religious end; a social purpose dominated. Experimentation in social programs—the introduction of kindergartens, playrooms, and so on—often required training which was alien to traditional church work.[86] In short, the nonreligious purposes of charities would demand expert (perhaps professional) personnel who would be trained to understand and achieve new ends which had to fit into a larger plan, a science of charity, a science of society.

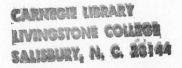

NOTES

1. Barton J. Bernstein, "Francis Greenwood Peabody: Conservative Social Critic," *New England Quarterly*, XXXVI (September 1963), 320–337, is the best brief analysis of Peabody's thought.

2. Francis G. Peabody, "Unitarianism and Philanthropy," *Charities Review*, V (November 1895), 25–32.

3. Daniel T. McColgan, *Joseph Tuckerman: Pioneer in Social Work* (Washington, D.C., 1940).

4. Thomas Chalmers, *Works* (Glasgow, 1836), XXI, 101-112; Thomas Chalmers, *Christian and Civic Economy of Large Towns* (Glasgow, 1821–1826), II, 140 ff.; Nevil Masterson, *Chalmers on Charity* (Westminster, 1900), 207, 288–289, 306 ff.; Frank D. Watson, *The Charity Organization Movement in the United States* (New York, 1922), 33–38; Grace Chalmers Wood, *The Opinions of Dr. Chalmers Concerning Political Economy and Social Reform* (Edinburgh, 1912).

5. Chalmers, *Christian and Civic Economy*, 1, 53 ff., II, 55–61, 93; Wood, *The Opinions of Dr. Chalmers*, 63; Masterson, *Chalmers on Charity*, 288 ff.

6. Chalmers, Works, XVI, 225–234, 423, XXI 131–132; *The Opinions of Dr. Chalmers*, 70; Masterson, *Chalmers on Charity*, 331.

7. Roy Lubove, "The New York Association for Improving the Condition of the Poor: The Formative Years," *New York Historical Society Quarterly*, XLIII (1959), 307–327; Robert H. Bremner, *From the Depths: The Discovery of Poverty in the United States* (New York, 1964), Ch. 3.

8. Committee of Delegates from Benevolent Societies of Boston, *Report* (Boston, 1834) , 4–5.

9. Ibid., 6–9.

10. Ibid., 12–13.

11. Ibid., 14–15, 17.

12. Ibid., 8.

13. Ibid., 10.

14. Ibid., 23–25, author's emphasis.

15. Ibid., 26–29.

16. Benevolent Societies of Boston, *Annual Report*, I (1835) , 17, hereinafter cited as BSB.

17. Ibid., 7–8, 16–17, 25.

18. Ibid., 9–10.

19. Ibid., 27–28.

20. Ibid., 33, author's emphasis.

21. Ibid., 37, author's emphasis.

22. Ibid., and 40, author's emphasis.

23. Ibid., 41–42.

24. Ibid., 33.

25. Ibid., 33n, 34–35.

26. Fatherless and Widow's Society, Ladies' Relief Society, Mite Society, South End Sewing Circle, Howard Benevolent Society, Almoners' Society, Young Men's Benevolent Society, Seamen's Aid Society, West Parish Sewing Circle, Female Benevolent Society, Fragment Society, and the Dorcas Society.

27. See Society for the Prevention of Pauperism, *Annual Reports*, hereinafter cited as SPP. This organization changed its name in 1871 to the Industrial Aid Society for the Prevention of Pauperism. Reports under the later name will be cited as IAS.

28. Boston Provident Society, *Annual Reports*, hereinafter cited as Provident.

29. Provident, Records of the meetings of the Board of Directors, December 8, 1853. These manuscript records are among the papers of the Boston Family Service Association.

30. Provident, *Report*, III (1854), 15.

31. Provident, Records, May 14 and September 16, 1857.

32. Ibid., March 4, 1858.

33. Ibid., March 1863, p. 218.

34. Provident, *Report*, XIX (1870), 11.

35. Ibid., XXVI (1877), 7–10.

36. Joseph Tuckerman, "Introduction," in Joseph Marie de Gerando, *The Visitor of the Poor*, 2d ed., tr. by a "lady of Boston" (Boston, 1833), xxvi–xxix.

37. SPP, *Report*, XXII (1857), 13–14, author's emphasis.

38. Allen F. Davis, *Spearheads For Reform: The Social Settlements and the Progressive Movement, 1890–1914* (New York, 1967), Chs. 1–2.

39. SPP, *Report*, XXVIII (1863), 6–7; Rev. Rufus W. Clark, "Discourse delivered before the Society for the Prevention of Pauperism, January 8, 1854," SPP *Report*, XVIII (1854), 22–23.

40. Ibid., XXIII (1858), 6.

41. Ibid., 7.

42. Provident, *Reports*, XXVIII (1879), 5–6; SPP, *Report*, XXXIV (1869), 7.

43. [G. Coolidge], "The Charities of Boston," *The Boston Almanac*, XXXVI (1871), 150–151.

44. Peabody, *Charities Review*, V, 32.

45. Bremner, *From the Depths*, 33.

46. William Ellery Channing, *The Obligation of a City to Care for and Watch Over the Moral Health of its Members; with Remarks on the Life and Character of the Rev. Dr. Tuckerman* (Glasgow, 1841). The following remarks by Channing are taken from this discourse.

47. Oscar Handlin, *Boston's Immigrants* (Cambridge, Mass. 1959), Chs. 1, 2, 4; Robert A. Woods, *Americans in Process* (Boston 1903), Ch. 1,

gives an excellent commentary on the demography of the North and West Ends. This latter work is hereinafter cited as Woods, *Americans.*

48. Edward Everett Hale, *If Jesus Came to Boston* (Boston, 1894), 3.

49. Ibid., 45.

50. *Lend A Hand,* VI (March 1891), 145ff.

51. Ibid., V (January 1890), 1–2, 4–5.

52. It is interesting to note the importance that both Hale and his son placed on these two magazines. *The Life and Letters of Edward Everett Hale,* ed. Edward Everett Hale, Jr. (Boston, 1917), II, 97–133.

53. *Lend A Hand,* IV (April 1889), 251–254.

54. Ibid., II (May 1887), 247–250.

55. Ibid., IV (August 1889), 551–554, and V (December 1890), 817-821, are among many suggestions to return to rural life.

56. Ibid., II (February 1887), 65-68.

57. Ibid., IV (December 1889), 845–848.

58. Ibid., V (August 1890), 521–526.

59. The village as an ideal social organization is one of Hale's most frequently expressed ideas in *Lend A Hand:* I (March 1886), 27–29, (May 1886), 253–255; II (May 1887), 247–250; III (August 1888), 429–431; IV (April 1889), 251–254, (July 1889), 477–482, (August 1889), 551–554; V (December 1890), 317–321—to mention a few.

60. Ibid., V (October 1890), 669–680. It is significant that the aims are wholly social. "This house will be, if you will pardon the word, the Cathedral of the ward. But I do not know why I use it, because it will set you off on the idea of preaching, which is the last thing I aim at" (670). "I call them ministers because that is just what they are; each of them, in his way and place, is to keep the run of his hundred families, and minister to them. But I do not want them to be preachers, more than I want the women in the settlement to be preachers, or men in the Cathedral. As I said before, there is preaching enough, and more than enough, taking the good with the poor." (675)

61. Ibid., III (October 1888), 551–554.

62. See comment on LeClaire, Illinois, in *Lend A Hand,* V (October 1890), 701–706.

63. Edward Everett Hale, Jr., *Life and Letters of Edward Everett Hale,* calls it "the great prevailing conception of his life and his work, and it resulted in the very sort of thing he had in mind" (II, 120). A general outline of the program and story is written by Rev. Christopher R. Eliot (II, 121–133; see 121*n*).

64. The story is in *The Works of Edward Everett Hale* (Boston, 1898–1903), III.

65. For impact see *The Life and Letters of Edward Everett Hale,* II, Ch. 23.

66. Peabody, *Charities Review,* V, 31.

67. Charles H. Hopkins, *The Rise of the Social Gospel in American Protestantism, 1865–1915* (New Haven, 1940), 116, 174, makes no distinc-

tion, but Henry F. May, *Protestant Churches in Industrial America* (New York, 1949), 207, notes that Hale's utopian novels depart from the pattern of the Social Gospel novelists; H. Richard Niebuhr, *The Kingdom of God in America* (Chicago, 1937), 194.

68. Historical summary can be found in Boston Port and Seamen's Aid Society, *Annual Report*, XXXIV (1901), 33–35, hereinafter cited as BPSAS. For origins see Boston Port Society, *Report*, XXIV (1852–53), 3–4.

69. For merger see BPSAS, I (1868), 3–4.

70. Comments on the extent of the Society's beneficence are in BPSAS, XX (1887), 10–11, and XXIV (1891), 11; also, Woods, *Americans*, 256.

71. Of the wife of Judge James Russell, Mrs. Annie Adams Fields comments, "of distinguished intellect—she has the savage element largely developed—a kind of freedom which she will never lose—a true child of Father Taylor and Mother Nature" (Annie Adams Fields, Diary, January 2, 1871, among the papers of A. A. Fields at the Massachusetts Historical Society, Boston, hereinafter referred to as Fields, Diary, and as Fields papers, MHS, respectively).

72. Boston Port Society, *Report*, XXIV (1852–53), 3, 4, 11; BPSAS, passim.

73. BPSAS, XVII (1884), 5–6.

74. Ibid., I (1869), 11, 15.

75. For shipping figures, see U. S. Bureau of Statistics, *Statistical Abstract of the United States* (Washington, D.C., 1879), Tables 133–142. Boston's shipping did not increase in proportion to other ports', nor did shipping keep pace with other growth in Boston. The BPSAS noticed the effects of cultural changes in the North End; see their *Report*, XX (1887), 6–7, and XXXIV (1901), 34–35: also, Woods, *Americans*, Ch. 1.

76. BPAS, XXXIV (1901), 8–9; the organization had in earlier years lobbied for legislation to aid sailors (XVIII [1885], 6–7, 11–12).

77. Cyrus Augustus Bartol, *Influence of the Ministry at Large* (Boston, 1836); Joseph Tuckerman, *A Letter on the Principles of the Missionary Enterprise* (Boston, 1831); Channing, *The Obligation of a City*, 11–24; Tuckerman, *The Principles and Results of the Ministry-at-Large in Boston* (Boston, 1838), and also his "Introduction," *Visitor of the Poor*.

78. Benevolent Fraternity of Churches, *Annual Report*, LXVII (1901), 3–4, for a general history; XXXVI (1870), 7–8, notices changes in the community and new needs; XXXVIII (1872), 39, notes missionary duties; LXVIII (1902), 27, on the North End Union.

79. Ibid., LXIII (1897), 35–36; Earl Christmas, *The House of Goodwill; a Story of Morgan Memorial* (Boston, 1924).

80. Benevolent Fraternity of Churches, *Annual Report*, LXIII (1897), 25–26.

81. Robert A. Woods, *A City Wilderness* (Boston, 1898), 263–264, hereinafter referred to as Woods, *City*.

82. The North End Mission, for instance, began to extend its work in 1880 (North End Mission, Records, November 1880, among the papers

of the Children's Aid Association, Boston). By 1908 the North End Mission had changed the name of the officer from Missionary to Superintendent (Records, December 1908).

83. Woods, *City*, 208–213; Rev. Frederic B. Allen, "Historical Address," Episcopal City Mission, *Report* (May, 1919); Woods, *Americans*, 262–267 (need for work among Negroes, 261–262; impotence of Protestantism, 363–364). Problems of lack of parish discussed in Woods, *City*, 226. The "institutional" church during this period see William W. Sweet, *The Story of Religion in America* (New York, 1939), 524–527, and Clifton E. Olmstead, *History of Religion in the United States* (Englewood Cliffs, N.J., 1960), Ch. 24.

84. Davis, *Spearheads For Reform*.

85. Charles R. Codman, draft of a note to his children, dated Christmas Eve, 1889, among the papers of Charles Russell Codman at the Massachusetts Historical Society, Boston, hereinafter cited as Codman papers, MHS.

86. The Old South Congregational (Unitarian) Church taught Froebel to those who wanted to attend classes. Letter from Edward E. Hale to George(?), dated January 27, 1897, among the papers of E. E. Hale in Houghton Library, Harvard University, hereinafter cited as Hale papers, Houghton.

3

Charity Organization
in Boston

THE principles and methods of charity were much debated
in the years before the Civil War, but the long-sustained
crisis of the 1870s fully tested existing methods and forced
reform. Two shocks, one upon the other, forced Bostonians
toward a reassessment. A fire which began on November 8,
1872, continued for several days and consumed much of Summer Street in Boston. The property loss was high, some estimated as high as $75 million, but the severe damage to the
garment industry compounded the cost by adding unemployment to the distress. The small wages that had been drawn
from these workrooms were lost to labor. The displaced
working men and women could not be absorbed elsewhere
but had to await the garment industry's recovery. The second shock, economic depression, was at first almost unper-
ceived, but its effects continued throughout the decade and,
at last, were to prove most telling.

The spectacular fire drew immediate attention. Organizations and individuals turned energetically to the task of relief. Fire committees, the Provident and other organizations

set up special funds, and private citizens gave their time to relieve distress and reestablish workrooms. But it was not until midway in the decade that people became aware that something more had occurred than a fire with a few business failures, that something more than generosity was demanded, and that perhaps a new concept of relief was needed.[1]

By 1874 there were renewed efforts to coordinate charitable activities. Edward Everett Hale called a meeting of delegates, which came to nothing, and a new organization, the Boston Bureau of Charity, failed to win the approval of existing agencies.[2]

Although jealousies prevented cooperation, the extraordinary cost of relief could not be ignored. The bill had to be paid by public subscription, and necessarily there had to be a justification and reassessment of methods. Annie Adams Fields, who was to become a principal leader of Boston's reform, gave her support to an appeal for funds by the Boston Provident Association; it was a qualified support, however. The high cost had not been due to the extravagance of the Provident. The money had been "painfully and carefully distributed in small sums ranging from $1 to $3 in the form of groceries and shoes." While Bostonians might regret the high cost of relief, she added, they "ought to be grateful . . . for having so much hard work done" for them. Still, it all meant that everyone would be deprived of some luxury or comfort.

Yet, she asserted, the debt had to be paid; it was a "debt of honor as well as charity." But after this civic duty is performed, she asked, "does not an equal obligation rest upon the public of reflection upon the subject whether so large a sum as twenty-five or thirty thousand dollars may be better employed than in giving food and clothing to the healthy poor because they cannot get work?" Half of the sum that the Provident expended would always be needed to "succor the sick and unfortunate and as we become more systematic and careful . . . the amount will increase somewhat with the growth of the city." She thought the present situation, however, to be impossible; some hard work had to be done to bring about reform.[3]

A few Boston ladies, along with Mrs. Fields, were prepared to work. They were in a tradition of middle-class English and American women who had devoted their ample leisure to social reforms—prison, abolition, education, temperance, women's rights—charities was to join the list. Women like Mrs. Fields in Boston, Louisa Schuyler, and Josephine Shaw Lowell in New York were especially anxious to remove the "lady bountiful" epithet that stigmatized their sex in charity work. They stand in sharp contrast to Jane Addams, whose personal wealth in the midst of wide human suffering quickened a sense of guilt which she could overcome only by profound respect and sympathy for the poor.[4] Unlike Miss Addams, the ladies of charity reform indulged little sense of their personal limitations. These ladies were heartened by the work of the Englishwoman, Octavia Hill, who in 1864, under the tutelage of John Ruskin, managed a successful experiment in housing for the poor in East London slums. Miss Hill's work used personal visitors, rather than rent collectors. Her several pamphlets tried to justify the personal, but pragmatic and vigorous, approach to work with the poor that Thomas Chalmers and Joseph Tuckerman had suggested. Here was a means for women to do constructive work with the poor without succumbing to soft sentiment.

With all of her eagerness, it was not until the summer of 1875 that Mrs. Fields found something that she could do. At her summer place at Manchester, Massachusetts, she and Mrs. James Lodge began discussion that led to the formation of the Cooperative Society of Visitors. They had received from Louisa Schuyler the collected pamphlets of Octavia Hill, which they hoped would guide them in organizing their own group. Outside the pamphlets Miss Hill was of little help. "For I shld. be wrong," she wrote, "if I tried to apply principles to special cases . . . & the principles I have I think put down in print as well as I can do."[5] By the end of the summer the Mesdames Fields and Lodge not only had a plan, but they had a list of visitors as well.

Mrs. James Lodge and Mrs. James T. (Annie Adams) Fields became president and vice-president of the Cooperative Society of Visitors. There were no new principles here. Like the defunct Association of Benevolent Societies, it too insisted on investigation, personal visitation and *"charity in the form of work."* To this last point the ladies gave the greatest stress. They established workrooms, put girls to work and tried to find or create jobs for able-bodied men. They were reluctant to give any relief in money or goods.[6]

The Society, however, departed from earlier reform ideas in recognizing the need for special skill in charity work; the voluntary visitor was not enough. They brought from Octavia Hill the idea of district committees as study groups— each visitor was to learn from the experience of others. This committee idea actually questioned the volunteers' competence. Demanding a full-time agent, it contained the germ of the idea of a paid, trained worker. They anticipated, earlier than is generally supposed, the limitations of the volunteer in charity work. The volunteer was too subject to sentiment and confusion. "It is only by patient and skilful [*sic*] investigation we can get at the truth; therefore we need paid and skilled investigators."[7]

Thus, with the aspects both of a sewing circle for poor women and a charity organization society, the Cooperative Society did its work for a little over four years. After the formation of the Associated Charities in 1879 there was little reason for its existence. The new organization absorbed the old. Mrs. Fields became one of the Associated Charities' most active directors and creative minds. She did much of the planning, the hard work of enlisting volunteer visitors and staff personnel.[8]

"The *Aim* of This Society Is to Raise the *Needy* Above the Need of Relief, But Not to Give Alms." Waving this banner line before, the Associated Charities presented itself to Boston and announced its objectives. The first and central idea of the Associated Charities was cooperation: "to secure the concurrent and harmonious action of the different charities of Boston." They hoped to raise the poor above relief, "prevent begging and imposition, and diminish pauperism." Thrift, self-dependence, and industry were to be encouraged through "friendly intercourse, advice and sympathy." To do this the Association planned to investigate every applicant for relief, placing its findings at the disposal of benevolent individuals, charitable societies, and the Overseers of the Poor. Their aim was employment if possible, "if not . . . so far as necessary, suitable assistance for every deserving applicant." All relief, whether by alms or charitable work, was to be made "conditional upon good conduct and progress." Ideally, the needy would "*graduate* from the rolls of relief, and their children be prevented from falling into need."[9]

The Associated Charities established district conferences which roughly corresponded to city wards. The membership of each conference represented the widest range of public and private agencies in the district: Overseers of the Poor who lived there, visitors who worked there, all public officials who served its poor, representatives of its other charitable or church societies, the district's captain of police.

Each conference had weekly meetings to discuss the distribution and handling of cases. They elected an executive committee which organized, controlled, and advised voluntary visitors; passed intelligence on to the central office; hired an agent for the district; and saw that each applicant was investigated.

The conference sent three delegates, including its president and secretary to the Council of the Associated Charities. There they joined their like number from the other district conferences and other public and private officials: the Mayor, the State Superintendents of Indoor and Outdoor Poor, Inspector of State Charities, three Overseers of the Poor, one Director of Public Institutions, one Police Commissioner, one trustee of the City Hospital, the Superintendent of Police, and the City Physician. The Council, ignoring no possibilities of cooperation with other societies, provided ex officio memberships to the presidents of the Boston Provident, St. Vincent de Paul, the Roxbury Charitable Society, and "such other bodies as the council directs."[10]

The Associated Charities planned to make the district conference semiautonomous. Ideally, each contained enough intelligence to consider and dispose of most cases. The inclusion of representatives from public and private agencies made available to each applicant most community facilities. Such an inclusive conference also reduced the possibility of fraud and duplication of effort, as well as minimized organizational jealousies.

Many major cities similarly attempted to organize their charitable effort in these years. Their experiences differed, but all would have accepted the Boston Associated Charities as a model of charity reform. Buffalo could claim to be the first city to organize, but its main distinction was that the police department of that city kept a register of applicants for relief. Philadelphia set up thirty district conferences in 1878. Unlike Boston, however, these had little central control, and they were indifferent to cooperation with other agencies in the city. Under the leadership of Seth Low, one of the important names in the national reform, Brooklyn's program which was organized in 1879 stressed the maintenance of woodyards, laundries, and such means of work test. The urging of the State Board of Charities was necessary to get New York City's Charity Organization Society started in 1881. New York followed the Boston model with district associations and a strong central control through a unified treasury. Cincinnati had, in 1879, attempted to follow this model also but drifted into Philadelphia's style of decentralization until 1889, when it was reorganized. None of the cities which claimed reform societies, however, could match Boston's success in its program of volunteers. Boston's success may be due to the Associated Charities never having assumed that volunteers would be without what would later be called professional guidance.[11]

The Associated Charities of Boston's reception was not wholly cordial, despite its attempt to assure cooperation with the agencies. Robert C. Winthrop, president of the Provident Society, recognized the similarity of purpose of the two organizations. He found, in fact, their constitutions to be identical, "without a perceptible difference of addition or subtraction." There was some difference in machinery; "but, so far as the provisions of the new constitution pertain to the practical relief of the Poor, I have not been able to discover a single point which is not substantially and almost literally contemplated and provided for by our own Constitution and By-Laws."

Winthrop saw no need for the new association; it merely added to the already too numerous agencies for the poor. More than anything else, he saw the new organization as an affront to the Provident. If new methods of relief could be advanced, the Provident would have willingly adopted them. He would have been happy to bring the new people into the Provident so that they might put their ideas into practice. "I need not say how heartily they would be welcomed, and how gladly I should see one of them occupying the place which I must soon vacate." As it was, Winthrop insisted this new effort would merely spread the community energies and funds for charity among too many organizations. Before this new association passed itself off as an innovation Winthrop, as spokesman for the Provident and one of its elders, felt compelled to set the matter right. The Provident fathers had first announced these ideas, and Winthrop insisted on making that a matter of record. "I trust," he said, "we shall offer no obstacle or opposition to such a movement, . . . while we reserve for further deliberation the question of taking part in so multitudinous a Board of Supervisors."[12]

Apparently, Winthrop was not the only skeptic. Mr. Causten Browne, who had been with the Associated Charities from the first provisional meeting, looked back in 1898 and recalled how difficult those early years had been. "We had to fight our way to the favor of the existing charitable organizations of the city inch by inch." Browne could not recall anything which agitated Boston society more than the question whether the Associated Charities ought to be allowed to start. "I fear," Browne confessed, "that its friends were so active as to sometimes be considered social nuisances." He recalled a dinner in which he and a friend from the Provident disputed the issue around a portly, rich gentleman seated between them. "We fought as the Greek and Trojan heros fought for the body of Patroclus." As Browne recalled it, he won in the end. The old gentleman turned and said, " 'I believe I will give you a shilling' and the next day he sent me a hundred dollars for the good cause."[13]

Causten Browne remembered two standard objections to the new association. The first was a part of Robert C. Winthrop's general criticism: this newcomer was merely another claimant upon a general charitable fund, which was already too small to go around; and while the usefulness of the system of registration was recognized, it was the only valuable innovation and might cost more than it would be worth. The second objection touched more to the heart of the new method. Application of the new ideas, some believed, would make charity hard, Browne recalled. There was too much organization and machinery to permit the natural "beauty and sweetness of ministering to the poor." It was the system, the mechanics, that people objected to. "And they drew touching pictures of the poor man or poor woman suffering while the routine of reporting to the agent, and assignment of the case to the proper visitor was transacted."[14]

The charge of harshness was voiced quite often as the society became secure enough to assert its "new methods." The society's president, Robert Treat Paine, became extremely critical of the lenient methods of the Provident. Cautiously avoiding "putting in print any, even the slightest word, reflecting on the custom of the Provident to give injudicious doles," he felt compelled to write its executive secretary, Edward Frothingham, about it. Apparently, the Provident often gave small, weekly allotments of food, fuel, and clothes to poor families that included an able-bodied, though unemployed, adult. Paine referred to this as a dole and contended that such small sums should not be given at all. Able-bodied men and women should be forced to support their families. He had no objection, however, to larger sums being given to affect "constructive change." Paine lectured Frothingham and did not disguise his condescension: "I feel sure the Provident will take a new and strong (stronger than ever) hold on popular affection, when it fully accepts the duty (& privilege) of adequate & continuing aid to families of children dependent on worthy mothers—& conversely is reasonably firm in forcing drunken fathers to do their duty." Children should be taken away from unworthy families, at last resort. "This will *Save them from suffering*. Not that a multitude of children are to be taken away. . . . But the threat, the danger of it should be held up squarely before the eyes of the father."[15]

Frothingham's response was heated; he found it difficult to understand Paine's position. If Paine objected to the Provident's giving food, fuel, and clothes to poor families in accordance with their needs, if he criticized the giving of aid under the value of twenty dollars, then Frothingham would strongly disagree. The laborer's need of a ton of coal is just as worthy of consideration as the need of a "mechanic or clergyman" for twenty or fifty dollars. "For my part," Frothingham insisted, "whenever I hand a poor woman a $5 bill I don't call it a *dole,* but a *gift.*" Frothingham went on to object to Paine's arbitrary definitions. In fact, he claimed, those who received the largest sums were often most disappointing. He did not "advocate giving *anything,*" he concluded, "to men or women 'who are able to support their families' unless in times of misfortune when they are temporarily *not* able to support them."[16]

This dispute between the two societies was carried into the published reports of the Provident. They took issue publicly with the "modern reformers who would have us give nothing beyond what is absolutely needed, and not always that." The Provident would rather guard against the overcautious attitude which gives too little for fear of giving too much. The "manner" in which relief was given was the crucial issue. Oversuspicion by agencies was more likely to damage the self-respect of the poor than overdependence on alms. "Nor is it very likely," the report said, "that we shall make paupers by an occasional gift, judiciously bestowed, of something not strictly necessary, but which may be the means of making a poor family comfortable."[17]

Mistakenly, one might consider harshness the whole of this dispute. But the organizations' similarity in principles but difference in spirit fed the argument. It erupted two years later when one of the Associated Charities' district agents, Miss Frances A. Smith, tried to persuade Mr. Frothingham to take from the Overseers of the Poor the care of two pauper women. Miss Smith made a lengthy statement about the principles under which the Associated Charities operated. While not absolute rules, they were, she suggested, the guidelines of intelligent charity. With such a preface Miss Smith proceeded to explain why private charity (the Provident, in this instance), and not public agencies, should take care of old paupers outside of institutions. The people in her district took relief from the Overseers "as a right, and learn to depend upon this aid in youth, middle age, and old age as a legitimate source of income." According to Miss Smith, young people naturally ask, "Why should we join a saving society? the city will provide for us when we are old." Furthermore, public charity was more expensive than private because there was no reform demanded by public agencies. And taxing thrifty people to support the shiftless was neither a good example for young people nor fair to the industrious and virtuous.

Miss Smith conceded that the two organizations would concur about the advantages of private over public charity, especially where young people were involved. But was it not important for youth, she argued, to learn the necessity of providing for their old age? Was not this the true function of private benevolence? "Cannot this thrift be encouraged by benevolent societies and individuals taking the relief and aid of the aged into their own hands, granting it in such ways as shall most encourage the rising generation to grow up self-sustaining, even in their old age?"[18]

And Mr. Frothingham did prefer private over public relief. But he saw no application to the cases of two old women, Mrs. Boyle and Mrs. Early, who were "incapable of improvement." Nor could he understand Miss Smith's pedagogy. What did it matter whether private or public relief cared for such cases while they were outside of institutions? If they could not be gotten into almshouses, what difference would it make who helped them? "They are *helped* all the same, and the 'young people' know it, and will be just as likely to look forward to getting it in *their* 'old age' whether" the city or a benevolent individual does the helping. Everyone knew that large sums of money were given to the poor of the city. "Could the 'young people' be kept in ignorance of *that* fact, there might be some hope for them; but they read about it, and are perfectly familiar with it." Frothingham doubted that young people would be encouraged to depend on public relief merely because they saw a few old people receive it. They might just as well look forward to the almshouse as their final station. After all, he insisted, the mere sight of such "dirty, disagreeable, helpless old paupers" as these women going to the Overseers was repulsive enough to any right-minded person. Indeed, should it not keep them from "going to Chardon St. at all, much less from counting upon going thither 'in their old age?' " No, Frothingham was quite willing to let public relief take care of such irremedial cases in order that private funds would be free to do constructive work.[19]

Clearly, Miss Smith saw charity as a lever or, rather, a goad, to individual reform. As long as it remained in the hands of private agencies, private individuals could affect personal improvement. Statutory provisions, however, would disarm the private citizen and render him powerless to restrict the growth of pauperism in the community. It is difficult to say how Miss Smith would have managed the care of Mrs. Boyle and Mrs. Early. Perhaps she would have made each grant of aid difficult, and, so harassed, they would have to leave the community or raise themselves from pauperism. However she would have used it, charity was to be a weapon in her hands. The same attitude can be noted in Paine's criticism of the Provident's "injudicious doles." He saw that by giving or refusing to give, one could affect individual reform. Frothingham, on the other hand, merely wanted to relieve need efficiently. He recognized the danger of dependence; he was willing to stop aid at some point. Yet he did not see charity as an instrument of social reform as did Miss Smith and Mr. Paine. The Associated Charities must have seemed to Frothingham extraordinarily harsh and arbitrary; not merely in Causten Browne's sense of slowness, but harsh and cold rather in the sense of a science.

While the continued dispute raged over method, spirit, and intent of charity, one suspects that jealousy was at the heart. So, by the end of 1885, when the Provident was being criticized by the press, it immediately suspected the source. "I have strong suspicion of the Asso. Charities," Francis E. Parker wrote; the "Revd. E. E. Hale was inaccurate by nature and habit. This report must be set right."[20]

Despite this petty bickering, the Associated Charities became an accepted institution. Taking onto its board of directors officers from the major city charities had lessened its threat to the older organizations. Also, the Associated Charities' connection with the charities organization movement made it a leader of national reform. Since the Associated Charities gave no money, it depended on established organizations; thus it sustained their function. And the Associated Charities used its influence to support other reforms, from the Anti-Tenement House League to immigration restriction.[21] By the end of the century people were willing to believe that it was something good in charity, whether or not they were willing to accept it as new.

The charity organization people, however, were convinced they had a new idea of giving. The "old charity," they thought, merely increased the dole as the need increased. "The only idea of the Old Charity is bread, more bread, soup, more soup. If there is one beggar, one loaf. If two beggars, two loaves. . . . A thousand poor, one soup-house; two thousand, two soup-houses." This idea clearly did nothing to solve the problems of the poor. The new charity, however, was remedial: "The Old Charity sees a woman begging, having in her arms a child with diseased eyes, distorted legs, festering sores"; it gave her what she asked for, money or food. It "thereby puts a premium on diseased, distorted children; and so such children were made to order by the thou-

sands, while the Old Charity goes away hugging itself over
its tenderness of heart." The "New Charity," on the other
hand, treated the child, sent the woman to jail, and removed
"all inducement for the production and exhibition of distorted children."[22] Indeed, the new idea was that soup, bread,
clothes, and fuel did not constitute charity at all. True charity had to improve the person. And this could not be done
by bread alone.[23]

Ideally, a man had to be involved in his own improvement.
"Their [Organized Charity] methods are moral as distinguished from physical; that is, if a man wants bread he must
first be fed and afterward shown how he may earn his own
bread in the future for himself." And, to this end, the efforts
of society as a whole had to be directed. Organized charity
wanted everyone, benevolent individuals as well as societies, to conform and to lend a hand. "The significance in
short," Mrs. Fields said, "of the words 'Associated Charities,'
is to interest well-to-do people in behalf of their poorer
neighbors."[24]

These ideas were more anxious statements of what had
been said some sixty-five years earlier in Glasgow. And they
had been part of the thinking of charity reformers in Boston
from 1830 on. As Robert C. Winthrop would have been
quick to point out, the "new charity" was slightly worn, and
many of its methods were, in fact, old hat.

The Associated Charities had, however, a spirit which was
new. It may have been the knowledge that charity organization was a national movement supported by English experience, or it may have been some special fear born of the depression of 1873; whatever, the people in the movement
talked and acted like innovators, reformers, and crusaders.
The new spirit was their sense of moral necessity, but without the religious imperatives of an earlier age.

The charity reformers were heirs to Thomas Chalmers'
distinction between pauperism and poverty. They limited

their task to controlling pauperism. It was naive to expect
more, for, after all, "the poor ye shall have with ye always."[25]
The reformers also echoed Chalmers' criticism of statutory
relief. Wherever there were alms there would be requests
for them. Public laws, therefore, made relief a right and created its own demand. Every tramp knew, it was claimed, that
there was free soup in every station house in Boston. Not
that he would come to Boston with soup in mind as subsistence. "But it would be true to say that he goes to Boston
with the feeling . . . that he shall not starve to death when
he gets there." Assurance of care made men less than self-
reliant, it was claimed. "If it is known that there is a loaf
to be had for nothing, ten men will quit work in order to
get the offered loaf." Thus their attack on indiscriminate
relief was two-pronged. The public authority must limit its
outdoor relief and the private agency and individual must
channel their philanthropy to intelligent and constructive
ends.[26]

In keeping with the reformers' questioning of public outdoor relief was an attempt to reassess institutional care. Demand for the reform of institutions was especially widespread
in these years. The proceedings of the National Conferences
of Charities and Corrections contained lengthy discussions
on the subject almost every year. And at the same time public
agencies, especially through the Massachusetts Board of Charities, was bringing a rational order to its various asylums and
houses of detention and correction. One article in *Lend A
Hand* reported a Cardinal Wiseman to have criticized Protestants for hiding their poor in institutions, out of sight and
mind. He had held that the poor should be visible, even if
they were beggars. "Let men and women who are prosperous,
be reminded that prosperity is not the only law. Let men and
women who have duties, be reminded of those duties by
daily contact with the poor for whom they are to be rendered."[27] The author of this article was impressed by Car-

dinal Wiseman's complaint that institutions should be a last resort. As long as there was hope of self-help, people should be kept away from institutions. This applied to children especially. Institutions limited personal care; they inhibited reform.[28]

The care of persons within or without public institutions could no longer be merely a matter of good intentions. The new era of charity was to be one of "sub-divided labors and coordinated energies . . . akin to that which had already taken place in the industrial world," D. O. Kellogg proclaimed.[29] And with new organization and new methods would come "the *data* for an inductive treatment of social problems"; they made an "experimental science possible."[30] Collection of data was important to the reformers. Statistics became a magic device which would uncover the source of crime.[31] They would contribute to the general knowledge: "A body of information is thus being created," the Children's Aid Society reported, "from which may come the enrichment of the whole programme of preventive effort."[32]

But more than this, the emphasis on statistics assumed a natural law determining social action; to do good one needed science rather than sympathy. The individual whim must be restrained, for an error in judgment, "be the motive never so high and unselfish, will revenge itself upon the innocent." Private sentiment had to be subordinated to science even though we might be "shocked by the hardness of these social laws as science states their limits and conditions."[33]

This emphasis on science as an instrument of reform distinguished the new charity reform from the old of Chalmers and Tuckerman. The statistics had a coldness about them and, coupled with the recognized complexity resulting from urban growth, caused many benevolent individuals to worry that impersonality would result from the reform.[34] The reformers' answer was that the volunteer visitor would continue to supply the warmth and friendliness while acting under the aegis of organized rationality.

The Associated Charities reiterated the notion of visitors establishing friendly relations between the rich and the poor. "It was only through familiarity with their lives at home, through standing on really friendly terms with them, that any successful attempt could be made to improve the conditions of the very poor."[35]

While there was no general agreement as to what this friendship should be, the volunteer's work was thought to be moral. Since the causes of "ninty-nine out of a hundred" cases of depravity lie within the man himself, "our aim should be to elevate . . . the man's nature; to speak the word of hope that shall arouse him from his lethargy and despair; to stand beside him as a friend." Because it was a moral work, it was naive to look for immediate signs of success or failure; this was a long-time job. "We shall never be successful 'Friendly Visitors,' until we are willing to leave out of the account the question of success or failure."[36] To some, the moral act was the mere bringing of the rich and poor together. " 'A friend' is the best preventative and cure of individual pauperism; and that part of society which is intelligent, virtuous and prosperous must everywhere and always make itself the friend to that other part which is ignorant, vicious or miserable."[37] For some, this friendship was to direct the poor to resources in the community which would help him help himself; make him educate himself and his children; make him use existing community resources.[38]

And the friend was sometimes thought to be an educator. Impressed with the "housekeeping ignorance and incapacity of working women generally," some visitors found that they had to "teach these heads of families the alphabet, at least, of household economy, as the first step toward comfort."[39] The conception of the visitor as an educator sometimes gave to the matter the harsh edge of master rather than friend: "Let us take the little child in the future," wrote Annie Fields, "from its possibly ignorant, filthy, careless mother, as soon as it can walk . . . and give it three hours daily in the kindergarten, where during that time it will be made clean, will enjoy light, color, order, music and the sweet influence of a loving and self-controlled voice."[40]

Yet, against this vague searching to define how voluntary work could scientifically achieve the end of reform, there was always the misgiving that a professional detachment was inevitable unless special steps were taken. Within the camp of the charity reformer could still be heard the voice of Lady Bountiful: "Here in this city are probably fifty women," one reformer asserted, "some are widows and some have never been married, who do not have to struggle for their daily bread." These women would be happier with some definite work to do, "more difficult than sewing a garment for a missionary, or carrying a dinner to a poor family." Why not, it was asked, organize such women into a sisterhood? If they could be trained and detailed for "two or more weeks' service twice or three times in a year, you would have the ideal hospital nursing." Of course, the sisterhood would receive nothing for their service. And, of course, the heavy work "such as washing, etc.," would be "done by the ordinary hired help."[41]

So the charity organization people were confused. On the one hand, the reform was a reaction against the Lady Bountiful and an effort to make relief more rigorous and scientific, while on the other hand there was always the sentiment that detached and professional organizations could never meet the true needs of the poor. By dividing the city into districts, allowing the visitor to work with groups of other visitors in his district and placing in charge a paid agent, the Associated Charities attempted both—keeping the personal qualities of volunteer work while it controlled the benevolence of the visitor. Ideally, the visitor had only two cases. He was not to be overworked. He was encouraged to be close and intimate with his families; he was to try to be a friend. It was suggested that he might divulge some of his own problems.

The poor had to have faith in the friendship before they would take advice for their own uplift.[42]

The intimacy of the relationship between the visitor and the family was always stressed above everything else. Friendly visiting was not merely wise relief-giving. It was not merely finding employment, or getting children in school and training them to skills, or improving sanitary conditions, or teaching economical cooking or buying, or enforcing habits of thrift. According to Mary Richmond, student of Zilpha Smith of the Associated Charities, it could have been a little of all of these, but more. It was "intimate and continuous knowledge of . . . a poor family's joys, sorrows, opinions, feelings, and entire outlook on life." With this, a visitor could not blunder, Mary Richmond claimed. But without it, he would be in serious trouble.[43]

The intimacy of the visitor permitted him to make demands on the family for its own self-help. Mary Richmond suggested that all relief should be coupled with some demand for the poor's improvement. "If outside help is needed, it should be made conditional upon renewed effort at work or in school, upon willingness to receive training, upon cleanliness, or upon some other development within the family that will aid in their uplifting." Nor were these conditions to be made in order that relief be difficult. Rather they were to use "relief as a lever . . . we should make our help a ladder rather than a crutch . . . every sensible reasonable condition is a round in the ladder."[44] And because of the visitor's close association with relief agencies and sympathy with the family there could be certainty that the right relief was forthcoming as long as needed. For it was recognized that the next demoralizing thing to pauperism was dependence upon uncertain and spasmodic charity.[45]

Because of the conference idea, the visitor did not work alone. Every Tuesday at three o'clock, the visitor met the conference and discussed special problems. The paid agent generally had some report to make and was always available to advise the volunteer. The conference meetings were designed to give the visitor a larger perspective, to allow individual problems to be seen in relation to others. And when the visitor was confused as to what to do next, some suggestion should come from the group. Of course, visitors did not have truly incorrigible people, so the possibility of discouragement was reduced.[46]

The conference was more than a seminar for volunteers. It brought together all of the data of the cases in its district; the compilation of these data for the whole city gave the Council of the Associated Charities the statistical accumulation that they understood to be essential to scientific method. Each year, with the Annual Report, the Associated Charities published its statistics. Rarely was there any interpretation; the figures alone seemed to justify themselves. When, in a year like 1881, the report on registration alone showed that the Associated Charities uncovered 14,518 duplications out of 33,448 names reported, no additional interpretation was needed.[47]

Other figures were more difficult to understand. The categories themselves, however, are instructive of the intent of the Associated Charities. Broad categories were the outline of these statistics, indicating the Association's expectation of change:[48]

I. CONDITION WHEN RECEIVED

Worthy of Relief:
Orphans with no parents, or one parent unable to support them
The aged
The incurable
Temporary illness or accident

Needing Work Rather Than Relief:
Out of work, able, and willing

Insufficient work, able, and willing to do more

By infirmity or family cares unfitted for all but special kinds of work

The shiftless, improvident, or intemperate who are not yet hopelessly so

Unworthy, Not Entitled to Relief:
Having property
Relatives able to support
The shiftless who seem permanently so
The improvident and vicious who seem permanently so
Those who prefer to live on alms
Tramps
Confirmed intemperance

II. CONFERENCES TREATMENT OF CASES

Number assigned to visitors
Number of visitors
Families moved to better tenements
Sent out of city where they would be self-supporting or where relatives could care for them
Families broken up to save children
Frauds exposed
Begging prevented
Progress made toward:
    economy
    neatness
    temperance
Families who have become self-supporting
Families who have saved money
Families aided to obtain skill made self-supporting thereby
Families started in business made self-supporting thereby
Families for whom work has been procured
    temporary
    permanent
    charity work
    other work
Procured pardon of breadwinner out of House of Correction

III. PRESENT STATE OF CASES

Families that are self-supporting
Families that are self-supporting but will need supplemental
     aid
Partly self-supporting
Partly dependent, but ought not to be
Wholly dependent and must for the time remain so
Wholly dependent, but need not be
Wholly dependent, but will soon be self-supporting
Helped, but should not be
Drunken or immoral persons, needing legal action
Others, whose present condition is unknown (chiefly with-
     out visitors)
Wholly supported by relatives and friends
Cared for by relatives, friends, or societies (NOT inde-
     pendent of visitors)
In homes
In House of Correction for begging
Dead
Not classified

The figures fell into these categories; proving what? The
Association did not publish an interpretation of the data;
doubtless they felt it unnecessary. Their commitment was to
the idea of numbers and categories. Theirs was a science of
description, not of analysis. Classification was quite enough
because their assumptions were never in doubt. They had
not questioned the principles of Tuckerman and the earlier
reformers. They merely used numbers to emphasize the
urgency of reform.

They did not need to convince themselves that close to
half the applications for charity could be eliminated by the
removal of duplications. They did not need to count noses
to see a correlation between intemperance and pauperism.
They did not have to await the polls anxiously to know that
many dependent people could be made self-supporting. They

knew these things already. They knew them so well, of course, that their statistics became mere reiteration. While the numbers might not have had a "scientific" purpose, they served to impress the community with the reformers' truths.

Thus the Associated Charities of Boston, leading in many instances the national charity organization movement, combined the moralistic charity of the past and the scientific spirit of the time. While they often spoke of the voluntary visitor as central to the reform, it is quite clear that the reformers abandoned pure volunteerism. Here was a new, organized, rationalized, scientific approach to social problems. Although they chose to continue to speak the language of the amateur, they were defining the skills and the attitude of the professional.

NOTES

1. Fatherless, *Reports*, LVI (1873), 5; SPP, *Reports*, XXXVIII (1873), 6–7, and XXXIX (1874), 7; Provident, *Reports*, XXIII (1874), 9–10; Fields, Diary, November 10, 21 and December 1, 1872.

2. Provident, Records of the Board of Managers, March 6, 1874. These manuscript reports are among the papers of the Family Service Association, Boston, hereinafter cited as Records.

3. Annie Adams Fields, Draft of a letter with no addressee, dated 1875. among Fields papers, MHS.

4. Christopher Lasch, *The New Radicalism in America, 1889–1965* (New York, 1965), Ch. 1.

5. Fields, Diary, August 12 and 17, 1875, and October 21, 23 and 25, 1876; letter from Octavia Hill to Annie Adams Fields, October 26, 1875, among Fields papers, Houghton Library, Harvard.

6. Cooperative Society of Visitors, *Report* (1878), 18.

7. Roy Lubove, *The Professional Altruist: The Emergence of Social Work as a Career, 1880–1930* (New York, 1969), 16–18, hereinafter cited as Lubove, *Professional Altruist*, assumes other reasons for failure of volunteers.

8. Letters from Annie Adams Fields to Richard H. Dana, November 7, 12, and 13, 1878, Fields papers, MHS.

9. Associated Charities, *Constitution of the Associated Charities of Boston* (Boston, December 9, 1879), 5–6.

10. Ibid., 6–8.

11. Charles D. Kellogg, "Charity Organization. . . ." NCCC, *Proceedings,* XX (1893), 52–93.

12. Provident, *Reports,* XXVIII (1879), 14–16.

13. Associated Charities, Records of the meetings of the Board of Directors, a copy of an address delivered on November 10, 1898; these manuscript records are among the papers of the Boston Family Service Association, hereinafter cited as Records. But the Associated Charities were warmly received by the IAS (*Reports,* XLIV [1879], 9–10).

14. IAS, *Reports,* XLIV (1879), 9–10.

15. Letter from Robert Treat Paine to Edward Frothingham, March 19, 1887, among the papers of the Family Service Association, Boston. See also letter from Charles P. Putnam to Provident, January 14, 1886 (among papers of the Family Service Association, Boston), which considers the Provident to be niggardly.

16. Letter from Edward Frothingham to Robert Treat Paine, March 23, 1887, Frothingham's emphasis. This is a manuscript copy of the original among the papers of the Family Service Association.

17. Provident, *Reports,* XXXI (1882), 11.

18. Letter from Frances A. Smith to Edward Frothingham, December 7, 1889, among the papers of the Boston Family Service Association.

19. Copy of a letter from Provident to Frances A. Smith, December 11, 1889, among the papers of the Boston Family Service Association; the copy is unsigned but in Frothingham's hand.

20. Letter from Francis E. Parker to Robert C. Winthrop, December 10, 1885, among the papers of Robert C. Winthrop in the Massachusetts Historical Society, hereinafter cited as Winthrop papers, MHS.

21. Associated Charities, Records, March 8, 1895, 80–81.

22. *Lend A Hand,* I (November 1886), 647, 690.

23. Ibid. (May 1886), 262.

24. A. A. Fields. "Lend A Hand, for 'Pain is not the fruit of Pain.' " *Lend A Hand,* I (January 1886), 7–8.

25. *Lend A Hand,* I (February 1886), 63–66.

26. "What Creates Pauperism," *Lend A Hand,* I (April 1886), 191–193. quoted pp. 191–192; I (March 1886), 185; public charity demoralizing (Provident, *Reports,* XXXVIII [1889], 10–11); public charity should be supplanted by organized charity (James W. Walk, "The Relations of Organized Charity to Public and Private Relief," National Conference on Charities and Correction, *Proceedings,* [1885,] 336–340, also cited in *Lend A Hand* I [July 1886], 389); notes stigma of public relief (Provident, Records, March 10, 1887, 177–178); pressure to reform city's Wayfarer's Lodge (IAS Executive Committee Reports, February 7, March 7, and April 4, 1898); Associated Charities effective propagating gospel of restraint in giving (Woods, *City,* 251).

27. "Public Institutions and Private Charity," *Lend A Hand,* I (November 1886), 639.

28. See regular discussions of institutional care in National Conference

on Charities and Corrections, *Proceedings*, hereinafter cited as NCCC. Also see letter from James Freeman Clarke to Edward E. Hale, March 29, 1875, among Clarke papers, Houghton.

29. D. O. Kellogg, "The Function of Charity Organization," *Lend A Hand*, I (August 1886), 452.

30. Ibid., see also SPP, *Report*, XXXIV (1869), 7–8.

31. Helen Campbell, "Criminal Geography," *Lend A Hand*, I (June 1886), 366–368.

32. Children's Aid Society, *Reports*, XXVII (1891), 9, hereinafter cited as CAS.

33. J. G. Brooks, "Social Question," *Lend A Hand*, I (January 1886), 11.

34. "Nobody Cares," *Lend A Hand*, I (July 1886), 415–416.

35. Mrs. James T. [Annie Adams] Fields, "Report to the Charity Conference of New York Women," *Lend A Hand*, I (February 1886), 101–103.

36. Anna L. Meeker, "Success in Charity," *Lend A Hand*, I (October) 1886, 598–599.

37. Fanny B. Ames, "Adequate Relief Versus Dole Giving," *Lend A Hand*, I (April 1886), 229–230.

38. "Notes on a Boston Ward," *Lend A Hand*, I (February 1886), 83–86.

39. "Woman's Work in Philanthrophy," *Lend A Hand*, I (March 1886), 156. The Instructive District Nurses considered it one of the major points of their service, the instruction of persons in a household to care for others (see Annual *Reports*, passim).

40. Fields, *Lend A Hand*, I, 8.

41. G. W. Shinn, "How the Lady Trustees Were Shocked," *Lend A Hand*, I (March 1886), 141.

42. Robert Treat Paine, "Address, delivered at the Charity Building on Chardon Street, Boston, March 12, 1879," Associated Charities, *Publication*, No. 6 (n.d., n.p.). Zilpha D. Smith, "The Education of the Friendly Visitor," NCCC (1892), 446.

43. Mary E. Richmond, *Friendly Visiting Among the Poor* (New York, 1918), 180; *The Long View, Papers and Addresses by Mary Richmond*, ed. Joanna C. Colcord (New York, 1930), 32, for influences of Zilpha Smith and Boston Associated Charities.

44. Richmond, *Friendly Visiting*, 190.

45. Ibid., 191.

46. Zilpha D. Smith, *Education*, 446–447; Robert Treat Paine, "Address," *Publication*.

47. Associated Charities, *Report*, II (1881), Appendix A, Table 2.

48. Ibid., Appendix B.

4

Reform in Child Care

THE new charity tried to combine theory and practice, simultaneously responding to principle and need. Reflecting the social and intellectual spirit of the late nineteenth century, private charities mirrored changes in religious sentiment, pragmatism, and the new scientism. Quite often, however, the reformers had to work against entrenched agencies and against habits of considerable maturity. This was certainly the case in the efforts to transform practices in the care of dependent children, especially as attitudes toward child care changed during the period. Mature institutions supposedly knew their business. It was no simple matter to show that they did not.

The establishment, in the early 1800s, of private asylums for the care of dependent children had been considered a reform of prevailing practices. Until then, except for rare instances of adoption, dependent children had been placed in state and county almshouses, where they mixed with every other kind of public ward. Maintenance had been the sole concern; the children were clothed, fed, and sometimes given the bare bones of an education. But, even these public in-

stitutions had become overcrowded. Private asylums, the answer for individuals who had been frustrated in finding a
place for children of their concern, were an improvement, if
only because they kept their charges away from the criminals,
insane, and paupers.[1]

But, by the last quarter of the nineteenth century, the
private asylums had become suspect to the new breed of
reformers. Three entrenched asylums—the Female Asylum,
the Children's Friend Society, and the Boston Asylum and
Farm School—presented problems that called for change.

The Female Asylum had been established in 1801. Its plan
had been to accept orphaned girls as wards and indenture
them at a reasonable age to private families for training in
domestic work. The contracting family was to be responsible
for the girl's room, board, medical care, and a fifty-dollar
settlement at her eighteenth year. This remained the Asylum's program until the opening years of the twentieth
century.[2]

Another asylum, supported by the Children's Friend Society, had been founded in 1833 to aid "exposed" children.
In this temporary hostel, the children were to be given an
"industrial" education with work around the house. The
variety and freedom of admission had been the original
justification for the establishment.[3]

A merger of two older societies had created the Boston
Asylum and Farm School. The Boston Asylum for Indigent
Boys (1814) had aimed to "rescue the most abject and for-
lorn, as well as those in the state of vagrancy who, roaming
from their parents . . . become old in the crimes of stealing,
swearing and lying." The Boston Farm School Society (1832),
on the other hand, had been established to help boys who
had been "exposed to moral evil" but who had not yet fallen
into the hands of the law. The two societies had joined in
1835 to establish a farm school on Thompson's Island in
Boston Harbor. There they had trained boys in farming as

well as such crafts as printing, shoemaking, and woodwork.[4]

By 1870 these institutions had exhibited faults that resulted from private direction to suit personal interest. Seldom had there been any direct relationship between the community's needs and the institutions' practices. No pattern had emerged that could define the principles governing admission, for instance. Training programs had not been designed to adapt to changing industrial needs. While the whim, caprice and ignorance of the directors sometimes had resulted in nothing more than nuisance, often the consequences had been tragic for the children and their families.

It certainly had not been changing community needs that prompted the Boston Asylum and Farm School to give up its policy of accepting delinquent boys. Juvenile crime in Boston had not abated. The decision to reject "vicious" boys and to accept only those with no fault but poverty merely marked a change in the directors' interests. The Boston Asylum had become willing to leave "reformation" to public institutions. Organizations that made such private decisions could not be relied on to meet the problems of the whole community which the new reformers sought to treat.

The admissions policies of these institutions had been determined by whim or sentiment; there had been no consistency. The Children's Friend Society, for instance, had claimed not to discriminate against the offspring of foreign parents. Yet it had refused Catholic applicants because the Protestant demand was large, and because it had thought the number of Catholic schools sufficient.[5]

The Female Asylum had been no better. Illegitimate children had troubled it greatly. It accepted one child because the "mother . . . had written a very repentant note." But it rejected another because "her influence would be injurious." Moral character had weighed heavily with this Board. It refused one girl because her cousin "has been committed to Sherborn for immorality," and her father had been considered immoral. Race, too, had confused it. A child of a white mother and a Negro father, "but with no trace of color in her appearance," was accepted, while the children of a Negro waiter who had worked at one job for eleven years but who had found it impossible to care for his girls after the death of their mother and grandmother, were refused. The only admission policy had been to avoid troublesome cases.[6]

The training that the children received also had been determined by the private assumptions of the boards of directors. Education had been, for the most part, vocational training—for the boys, farming or crafts; for the girls, domestic work.

Both the Female Asylum and the Children's Friend Society had always assumed that their girls' futures were assured in domestic service. As soon as a CFS girl had become old enough, the matron had trained her in "cooking, housework, and sewing." And at fourteen "each one follows the rule of three months in the laundry, three months with the chamber work, and three months in the kitchen; besides which she does her own mending." The Female Asylum also had tried to assure that their girls would "go well equipped for their work in life with a good knowledge of cooking and the other industrial arts of the household."[7]

This preoccupation with industrial training had not been wholly condescending. Chronic labor shortage in the first decades of the nineteenth century had insured jobs for trained young people. The Female Asylum had never had a shortage of requests for girls. "There has been a great demand for apprentices," they reported, "—so great—that we have often found it hard to decide upon the relative advantages of two or three places, where we had but a single girl to send."[8] But whatever the soundness of the original conception, these institutions remained wedded to their procedures far after new conditions had made them questionable.

Indeed, jealousy of program characterized these early agencies. The Children's Friend Society at one time had refused to continue an experiment of educating its children in the public schools, because it had placed a great burden on the matron to see that the children were properly clothed. But even more, the matron had to be mindful that "contact with outside influences quickens all the faculties; the activity of limb and muscle is increased, the appetite for food made keener, and above all . . . like other children, they are ready to learn the evil as well as the good." So too, the Female Asylum rejected an offer by Dr. Charles P. Putnam to have the girls taught typing. The ladies at the Asylum had "thought the children too young, and that also, if they were taught typewriting . . . it would unfit them for domestic services." They also declined an offer of a music teacher to give free lessons to an eight-year-old who had shown talent. And when the Asylum's teacher had taken it upon herself to train some of the girls in bookkeeping, the committee forced her to use her own time because her special training had been "encroaching on the time due to others."[9]

Such practices made these institutions vulnerable to the criticism that "the children . . . are generally trained into the very lowest grades of handiwork or domestic service";[10] the asylums, after all, had not dealt with individual talents.

Doubtless, the managers of these institutions had believed they were working in the best interest of the inmates. The Female Asylum's Board had often gone to great lengths to avoid injury to its wards. This organization had also demanded references from reputable persons in an applicant's community before indenturing a child. A girl could not be sent to a home with older boys or to one which took male boarders; she was to have proper and private sleeping accommodations. One member of the Board of Directors was to have "guardianship" of an indentured girl and was to see to her well-being.[11]

All the organizations had similar provisions. Yet, all

had made judgments which had been questionably in the children's interest. So, a former inmate could revisit the Children's Friend Society as an adult to learn for the first time that he had a sister who had been separated from him when he left the Home. And the Female Asylum often had confused the child's interest with its prescribed program. Thus their Committee could convince itself that a girl should not attend school because "Mrs. Sharon cannot spare her and thinks it bad for her to be with other children." Or, again, when New Hampshire passed a compulsory school law, forcing one woman to send her helper to school for part of the day, the Female Asylum had taken the part of the woman in insisting that the girl be let alone. The woman, after all, was not paying to have the girl go to school. The Female Asylum had tried to convince the New Hampshire authorities that the girl in question was "not bright and would have bad influence on the boys at school." New Hampshire was not persuaded, and the girl was brought back to be placed elsewhere.[12]

No amount of care and supervision could guarantee a healthy or satisfactory situation for an Asylum girl. Indeed, the records reveal that a problemless placement had been the exception. Sometimes the condition of the family changed, affecting the life of the indentured girl. In one such case the woman's husband had died, forcing her to work outside the home. The girl, free from adult supervision, soon became pregnant. More often, however, the Asylum was to make an error in judgment about the man of the house, later to be upset by complaints of his sexual advances to the girl. The pages of the records are filled with complaints of sexual misconduct by the husband, or sometimes the son, in the family. The girls often had to be moved four, five, or even eight times during their adolescence. In at least one case, parents had complained about a girl's "gross immorality" with their own children. They recognized that her wrongdoing was the result of "the bad influence and bad practices of the man to whom she was formerly bound." They had urged criminal action against him. But as "the Asylum had no proof of the man's wickedness, and only Lizzie's word to go upon, the managers, however indignant they might be against the wrong to the girl, did not feel that they could interfere in the matter."[13]

So with, perhaps, the best intentions, the growing girls of the Female Asylum had been moved from house to house that they might learn domestic skills. Removed from the direct oversight of the Asylum, alone in a strange family and subject to its commands, ignorant of sex beyond the teachings of their Victorian world, these little girls were vulnerable to whatever might compel the men in their households. It is little wonder that the reports of the Female Asylum are heavy with evidence of emotionally disturbed girls. They were often simply called insane. "She is not continuously insane but is subject to attacks of dementia." Most often problem girls had been explained as "feeble-minded." A handy label, it could not explain a girl's attempt to poison and gas herself.

The Asylum, nevertheless, had solved its problems simply, as with the case of one troubled girl who "is very sullen, wanders about the house at night frightening the children by appearing at their bedsides, is very untidy, & stays in the bath room for hours after she is persuaded to bathe herself." They had suspected that this girl had "bad habits, she hides away in dark closets & has to be constantly watched for fear she will take the younger children off with her." Whatever this girl's difficulty, she was sent to the home for the feeble-minded the following month.[14]

Undaunted, the Female Asylum, for the whole of the nineteenth century, had not brought its assumptions under serious scrutiny. Only once during the first hundred years had the Asylum considered revising its indenture or apprenticeship system. In 1844, the managers recognized that girls could earn a better salary before eighteen than the clothes, food, and shelter earned in apprenticeship. But this recognition had made the Asylum merely insist upon a money payment at the end of the indenture rather than any more fundamental revision of policy.[15]

Apprenticeship, however, was a vestige of a society of status and order, where mutual obligations and community cohesiveness could justify the unfreedom that it implied. It was among the many victims of the changes brought on by industry—which was freed from craft restrictions—and by a highly atomized society. Individuals in the nineteenth century became less bound to family, trade, and community. Therefore, the long-lived custom of binding children out—indenture— came much under question. While institutions such as the Female Asylum continued the practice, there was much confusion among all parties as to precisely what was entailed: Did the parent lose all legal right to the child after signing a surrender? Did the Asylum have full freedom to choose the child's future, its occupation, its future home, whether it should be returned to the parent? Did the indenture place any real obligations on the child? No satisfactory legal answers were given to these questions because there were no definitive court actions. Problems merely arose out of the confusion and were settled by chance. The uncertainty, itself, was merely another signal that the American concept of the child was undergoing important changes.

Sometimes misunderstanding resulted from a parent's ignorance of the conditions of "surrender" and the intent of the Female Asylum. One woman, for instance, had not understood that her girls were to be placed in families. She objected and asked for her children back. The Asylum reported that upon "inquiry it was thought to be unwise to allow her to have them, there being a question as to her character." This mother was even denied the company of her children during an illness. At last, after eight months, the matter of questionable character was cleared up: "a letter has been recently received from Mr. Bradley, superintendent of the Farm School at Thompson's Island, giving a much better account of the mother than that contained in a former letter from him." It was decided that the mother could have her children.[16]

In fact, however, the Asylum had been powerless to hold a child when the parent or the child had made a determined effort. One girl made so much trouble for the institution and her "foster" family that the Asylum was relieved to be rid of her. One mother forcibly removed her child from her situation, claiming that the girl had been sexually assaulted by the man of the family. She refused to allow the Asylum's doctor to examine the girl and was unmoved by the threats of a policeman who was sent to return the child. After a little effort the Asylum gave up.[17] In other instances where the mothers, considered unfit by the Asylum, had captured their children, the Asylum found the police impotent. In later years the Asylum did not make the effort.[18]

Yet the Asylum had persisted in attempting to determine the kind of home to which the child was to be released. If a mother remarried and thought herself able to care for her child, the Female Asylum would consider whether or not the new husband drank, whether the mother and her husband were moral—in short, whether or not it was a fit home. Sometimes this involved influencing the court to disallow the application for guardianship on the ground that the applicant "is called a fast-woman and is not considered fit to take charge of the children." And again, it could refuse the persistent requests of an "extremely unhappy" child to return to her mother, who wanted her. This refusal resulted in the girl's attempted suicide.[19]

In addition to these difficulties, the early child-care institutions had faced problems of health. The maintenance of children within the institutional walls had created special conditions. The slightest case of measles or mumps could assume epidemic dimensions if care were not taken. Sadly, the epidemics were rarely of simple childhood diseases; diphtheria and smallpox were common. They had been impossible to control. Despite precautions, sometimes entering children brought diseases with them.[20] Nor is it surprising, since sanitation and antisepsis were just being understood by the medical profession in the late 1880s. The Boston Lying-In was plagued by devastating epidemics of septicemia until 1887.[21] Often the asylums were assisted by the hospitals of the city.[22] The Instructive District Nurses, however, could not give special attention to institutions during time of emergency.[23] Grasping for a solution to the problem of epidemics, the Children's Friend Society finally moved its home into the country.[24]

Dissatisfaction with institutional care for dependent children became very evident by 1870. Often the criticism charged institutions with being operated according to the caprice and selfish ends of the trustees. Sometimes the trustees themselves, dissatisfied with closed, city-bound buildings, wanted to move the children into the open air and into family households. This latter view was becoming faddish through the efforts of Charles Loring Brace of the New York Children's Aid Society. But, doubtless, it was reflective more of the views of "Christian Nurture" that were being advanced by Horace Bushnell, the reform Protestant theologian.

It was always difficult for asylums to ignore public disinterest, evidenced in a contracting list of subscribers. They had to respond. All criticism insisted that institutions often had ignored the interests of the individual child and had sought to perpetuate themselves. The assumption that the individual dependent child had interests that deserved honor and attention is suggestive of the changes in child care that were underway. It became a commonplace statement that with "adequate supervision, the children themselves will be much better off in common average homes than in institutions, and the effect on the whole community is much better in every way." The reformers in charity observed that, especially after the generation of founders died, an institution's directors had been "apt to think that it exists so that it may exist. And they cannot understand that the perfection to be aimed at might be to empty wards and an Institution put up for sale."[25]

If the ends of charity reform were to be served in child-care organizations, an organization which was not institution-bound, which was devoted to the individual child, had to develop and assert itself. The Children's Aid Society, the agent of child-care reform in Boston, had had conventional beginnings. Nevertheless, it brought innovations in the methods of care of dependent children and convinced other benevolent organizations of the superiority of its new ways.[26]

The Children's Aid Society was founded in 1865 to help boys in minor difficulties with the law. Rufus R. Cook, the chaplain of the Suffolk County Jail, was the first agent of the organization. The plan, in the beginning, was simple. "Uncle" Cook tried to gain the release of boys to the custody of the Society. The Society assumed responsibility for the boy, demanding a release for a number of years from the child's parents. The boy would be sent to the organization's farm in West Newton, where he would be trained. During the first months the child was considered in rehabilitation, and he would be observed for signs of progress toward social adjustment. When the Society thought it proper he would be placed at some approved farm in New England. The farmer would then be responsible for schooling, clothing, and feeding him. At the end of the boy's probation he would be released.

The farm idea, as long as it remained, was kept very simple. The farmer taught the boys, retrieved them when they ran away and disciplined them when necessary. His wife managed the household, nursed sick boys, and taught school. In this "cottage plan"—a name assumed when other programs used it—the farmer and his wife were the heads of a Christian household. The boys were to learn by experiencing life in a proper family.

The idea was to reform the boys through Christian nurture rather than in some kind of "institution." There was nothing penal about the farms; "the boys have their liberty. They wear no uniforms." They could receive visits from their parents. "They find it a good Christian home, with the constant proofs of a hearty interest in their welfare. They should be kept there long enough to have these influences strike in, and the new color imparted become fast."[27]

The founders saw the farm not only as a means of teaching the boys a trade in a good family situation, but also as a means of getting them out of the city. There was something especially moral about the country and farming. The idea of reforming boys in the country, Robert Treat Paine claimed, was consistent with intelligent child care. The country had to be summoned to help the city, he asserted. "We cannot take care of these children and make good citizens out of them in Boston." They were subject to too many temptations. Child saving was an impossible task, Paine argued, "if it is only to be solved here or in other great cities."[28]

Of course, the boys were often close to another kind of reality. The city was all that they knew, or wanted to know. Indeed, sometimes the hope that the country would work its magic on the boys was wistful. The city persisted; "the malign attraction is recognized when they are away from the city. 'How I like the smell of that pipe; it smells so of Boston!' said a little fellow, the other day." It was true, after all, that after seven years, twenty out of ninety-five boys had run away.[29]

While the farm system remained the same over the years, there were some innovations. A home for girls was established in 1866, and the Society made every effort to adapt the program to meet their needs and interests. They met with unusual difficulties. The property was very decrepit. Improvement would have involved the Society in excessive expense. In addition, the "proper" kinds of girls were hard to get.[30]

Despite the obvious benefits of the country, the Society recognized it could not struggle against the tide of the city. They thought of establishing a home in the city. "Providence," it was claimed, "in our day will have great cities, and unless we would be found fighting against God we must care for the boys where many of them will be found as surely as 'all the rivers run to the sea.' "[31] But nothing came of this idea.

Recognition of industrial change was made in an attempt to establish an "industrial" home in Ludlow, Massachusetts, for those boys "old enough to work, but who prefer some other department of labor rather than that of farming." Six boys were sent to Ludlow under the care of a matron. The boys were to be employed in the factory there, "in work suited to their age and strength, with part of each Saturday for recreation"; their income was to defray the expense of the house. Thus, the boys would be learning jobs while under influences similar to those of Pine Farm. If the experiment proved successful, the numbers would increase to twelve. The experiment, however, did not succeed. "The boys became restless under the restraint of the long hours of work in the mill and could not be kept from the streets of the town in the evening." The management of the company which employed them became impatient with their neglect of work. And with so few boys it was difficult for the enterprise to pay for itself. The experiment was never attempted again.[32]

Since the Society's original intention was to save boys from penal institutions, it expected to receive "problem" cases. But these were by no means hardened criminals; the crimes for which they were charged were vagrancy, selling newspapers

without a license, and begging.[33] Although the Society never
lost its central interest in keeping boys out of reformatories,
there came a time when it wished to handle other than criminal children. By the end of the century it began to move in
new directions. While the Society was selective—it took only
children it thought it could help—it was not inclined to ex-
clude children on moral grounds. There were, to be sure,
some standard ethnic prejudices. One of the committee of
visitors to the girls' home, on seeing there a child of mixed
parentage, inquired whether it was the intention of the Directors to mix whites and Negroes, and "to take charge of
children of such an unnatural union." He thought that
white children should be preferred to Negroes in any case.
While Catholic boys at the farm were allowed to have a priest
visit, they were requested to attend religious services with the
rest of the boys: "the family unity would be broken, should
any of the boys leave the family place of worship on Sunday."
And with one incorrigible runaway it was thought "best to
let the Catholics look after him." But these problems seemed
rare in this organization. Its conception of itself as a society
for problem children seemed to work against petty discrimina-
tions.[34]

Significantly, the Children's Aid Society considered itself
an experiment from the beginning. This bias meant that the
organization was as free as possible of dogma. One idea dominated: institutions were bad, and the family system worked
wonders in reforming young boys. One visitor was impressed
with the difference between the Society's boys and those at
Deer Island. "There, the faces were blank, pale and sad—
here, they were bright, cheerful & healthy." The difference
was not in the boys; they were "precisely the same class who
go there, and who come to ours." Clearly, it was the superior
method. The insistence of this superiority was reiterated
throughout three decades.[35]

The experimental inclination of the Society was expressed
in continuous questioning. When should it give up a child

as beyond help? What advantage was there in gaining the legal control over boys? Some claimed that boys should be trained for a calling, that industrial skills should be stressed in the school. Others wanted to improve "the hearts & minds of the boys, & to make them healthy, happy, & good," to give them a general education including military drill and gymnastics. Still others saw the value of proper indoctrination. Because, it was thought, in "the present age of demagogues and professional labor agitators," it was important "that the early training of the laboring-classes should teach them to use their own judgment."[36] The Society tried to do all of these things. Continuous questioning led to innovation.

The Society wanted to care for problem boys. There was a kind of pride in this aspect of the work: "I repeat the suggestion of the visitor, for last month," said one man, "that we should have some active way of securing the boys otherwise destined to Marcella Str. or Deer Island & fill our vacancies with this class rather than with so many younger children." Yet, how to supervise and discipline such boys remained vexing. From the beginning the major problem was runaways. The farmer was ordinarily successful in recapturing the boys. Yet, what was to be done when they returned? The trustees were clearly against corporal punishment, so confinement of one sort or another was resorted to. Quite often the runaways were forced to remain in bed. But, obviously, that was not an adequate punishment. Many of the boys behaved well enough and were left for the "family" to punish through shame or lack of cooperation. The truly incorrigible were finally turned over to a state institution. One troublesome lad was placed on a farm and promised a fifty-dollar bonus if he behaved himself until he was eighteen; apparently, it worked with him.[37]

When a boy came to one of the farms he was taught agriculture by the older boys and the farmer. After a period of adjustment, he would be placed on a farm in New England. The Society laid down rules for the farmers who received the

boys, and in 1883 a person was placed on staff with the sole
responsibility to follow up the placement of the children.
Constant communications were kept with the boys by this
visitor, who made regular trips to investigate their situations.[38]

This was a simpler operation than that of the Female
Asylum. The farmer knew his responsibility for the boy's
intellectual and spiritual as well as vocational development;
the boys were to be accepted into the family. Needless to say,
there were abuses, yet the boys were not shifted around
nearly as much as the girls of the Female Asylum. Of course,
there were fewer problems with boys. Because the complaints
were never sexual, the relationship and the criticism were
more candid. The Society's visitor could find out that a boy
was overworked more readily than could a guardian get past
a girl's shame about a sexual act. Furthermore, the Children's
Aid Society's visitor was a paid agent, assuring uniform
reports.[39]

Thus, the Children's Aid Society's work with juvenile
delinquents was the beginning of modern work in probation.
At first, Rufus Cook was present at all sessions of the Police
Court and was on watch for boys he could help. "His system
of taking boys on probation by consent of the Court, instead
of, as formerly, having them sent to jail to await trial, has
worked most admirably." During 1866 Mr. Cook received
eighty-eight boys on six-week probation, and only four of
these had to be returned to the court. These probation boys
were "obliged to report to him, in person, every week at his
house, or at the Court, and so he is enabled to keep an eye
on them. It proves a constant check upon them and their
evident desire, in many cases, to improve is very gratifying."
Public agencies quickly recognized the success. Within four
years after the beginning of the organization, the State Board
of Charities could report that of nearly four hundred boys
taken by the Children's Aid Society, eighty percent were
doing well.[40]

But success brought new questions. What could be done with young boys who could not be placed on farms? For, after a short stay at the Society's farm, they would merely return to their bad homes and environment. Something was needed between farm labor and immediate release. "We wish the Society would authorize us to try the plan of paying moderate board to families in which we can trust" the younger boys, "and thus enable us to benefit a larger number." Why could not the Society pay persons to act as parents to individual children, thus eliminating the institution from child care altogether? The idea was not original with the Children's Aid Society. The suggestion had been made by a State agency a year earlier, but the CAS was to build its program around it.[41]

The Society's predisposition to experiment made many of its early activities preparatory for later programs. The habit of the visitors to the county jail of bringing books for the boys to read developed into home libraries for children in tenements in Boston. Likewise, the work with delinquents suggested to Mr. Cook that the Society could do good work before the boys had become subjected to legal action. In time, the Society extended its work to boys who were destitute but not bad, "for whom homes in the country can be provided but who do not need to be reformed before going to them."[42]

In 1886 the Children's Aid Society hired Charles W. Birtwell as an "outdoor agent." The illness and incapacity of Rufus Cook in 1884 and Birtwell's graduation from Harvard College in 1885 coincided to bring a change in management and policy. The transition was easy because the Society had been looking for a way to broaden its effectiveness, and Charles Birtwell had just the kind of energy, freedom from dogma, and willingness to experiment that could create a new program.[43]

Charles Birtwell began to work with children who, having been placed on probation by the courts, were returned to their former environments. Arguing that unless something

new was added to the equation these children would sooner
or later be returned to the court, he tried to find some way
for the Children's Aid Society to improve their lives. With
Society members acting as visitors, and often as probation
officers, they began to counsel these children and their parents. Birtwell also made use of existing agencies in the community. "He places them in industrial schools, evening
schools, sewing classes, etc., which otherwise, owing to the
ignorance and neglect of their parents, would not be used."
The child was sometimes placed at the farm or in a foster
home, depending on the condition of his own family. Besides
such programs, Birtwell tried to expand the Society's operation within its old context, finding more foster homes and
simplifying the investigation of children already placed
out.[44]

Typical of the new programs that Birtwell introduced was
the Home Library. The idea was simple. A visitor would
organize a group of children around a select library placed
in one's home. She would gather with these tenement children
to discuss the books, which were changed frequently for
variety. In the years before free public libraries became
common, this program provided a unique service. From the
visitor's point of view, however, these libraries were to do
more than provide good literature. Here was a good opportunity for uplift. And it was happily reported when the children in these literary groups showed virtues like punctuality
and thrift. One boy "carries and chops wood for an infirm old
man living near him; and two sisters help to take care of an
old woman who is ill." The genius of the program was that it
gave the children something to do while giving the visitors a
chance to direct their energies along socially acceptable
avenues.[45]

Thus the Society's program began to follow three lines:
work with children in their homes, placing out, and special
reformatory work at one of the Society's farms. The tendency

was to encourage a family to remain together. "It has always been borne in mind that the sundering of family ties—the separation of a child from a father or mother, or the scattering of brothers and sisters—is a serious matter, requiring for its justification grave reasons and evident advantages." If the child's own family was impossible, some other family was better than an institution. The Society's own farms, made as familylike as possible, were way stations where a child could be reformed sufficiently to go into a family or back to the community. Finally, the Society often referred children to other agencies in the city; indeed, Birtwell considered his organization a kind of information bureau for community child-care problems.[46]

Within this already diversifying program the Society found that it had great possibility of choice. It began to find families anticipating the adoption of children, families expecting some labor, and homes demanding all or part of the expense. The Society observed that most parents would make some effort to pay for their children's support, if they were given the opportunity; it insisted that parents always be given that chance to be responsible, even if the sum they were able to pay was negligible. Clearly, more funds would be needed to allow the Society to take full advantage of this diversity of program. The reports began to stress, therefore, its preventative as well as reformatory interests, encouraging its donors to give so that good boys could find good homes at the Society's expense. Also, referrals to other child-care agencies became a more important part of the organization's function.[47]

Diversification of program meant that the Society could more likely fit the particular needs of the child. With wide choice, the agent had to ask what was best for the child. The task of the Society, according to Birtwell, was to tailor its action to the individual child, heeding the teachings of experience. The agents were to "study the conditions with a freedom from assumptions, and a directness and freshness of view, as complete as though the case in hand stood absolutely alone." Thus, it was the child's "real need" which was served. The Society avowed its willingness to investigate, advise, and help any case of a needy child with a "naturalness of method." "We do not say we will do one thing and not another, but we stand ready to learn the need and, whatever it may be, to try either to see that others supply it or to supply it ourselves."[48]

This pragmatism was new in child-care agencies. It coincided, incidentally, with the growing pragmatism in the charity organization movement. The result was much the same. By 1900 the individual child and his need came to dominate the interest of the Society. By the end of the century the "case method" had become a conscious innovation. The "real need" of the child could only be learned by studying that child and his problem.[49]

The Children's Aid Society by the end of the century had supplanted its farm program with foster homes. The city had begun to encroach upon the farm at West Newton; it had to be given up, but it was difficult and expensive to find a suitable new location. Management of the farm was difficult since Mr. Washburn had retired. And it was impossible to find a man to act as father, farmer, teacher, disciplinarian, and retriever of runaway boys. Family heads are hard to hire, and even with the ideal Mr. Washburn it was doubtful that the farm could ever substitute for a family.[50]

Charles Birtwell continued through these years to refine techniques. New methods were devised to investigate prospective foster homes; definition and redefinition of purpose continued so as to know what kind of care the Society wanted to provide; refinements were made in care of children in their homes, so that the Society increased its effectiveness in the community.[51]

The Children's Aid Society's great influence in such national organizations as the National Conference on Charities and Corrections shows its leadership. Children's agencies in other cities and states adopted, in these years, much of the reform initiated by the Society. And within Boston, local organizations were coming around to reform. The prohibitive cost of maintenance of city institutions, the confusing indenture system, the frequency of epidemics, and the changing sentiments of trustees and the donating public combined to persuade many institutions to change their operations. By 1900 the Children's Friend Society had given up its asylum, and by 1909 the Female Asylum had turned to placing out. Both organizations, when time came to change, turned to the Children's Aid Society and Charles Birtwell for advice. The CAS, consciously a leader, gave freely of itself and its personnel.

The energy and imagination of the Children's Aid Society reflected the general public attention to child care during these years. "Child-saving," as they liked to refer to it, occupied much of the literature. The reformers were guaranteeing a better future by attention to children. The child, whatever one thought about adult paupers and the dangers of dependence, was the responsibility of the community. As the Reverend Phillips Brooks articulated the general sentiment, the child, after being the responsibility of the parents, is "the child of the State, of the community; then it is the child of this larger humanity which is represented in the community." Thus, when the primary relations fail the child "and the State comes forward in the person of you, its citizens, and folds its life about the child, and humanity comes forward in the person of you, its citizens, and folds its larger life about the child, it is not something unnatural and artificial."[52] This larger humanity was to be manifested in the community and in private activities of great variety. Everywhere there were new practical schemes reflecting the attitude of the reformers.

Of the many projects for the care of small children, the most interesting were crèches and kindergartens. The crèche was a means of caring for small children while the mother worked. Ordinarily supported by local churches, they served a dual purpose. They freed the mother to work—often the only source of support—and they cared for children who would otherwise be deserted during the day. Not merely a convenience to the parent, the crèches' purpose was reform through child care. Serving much the same purpose was the free kindergarten movement. First championed by Elizabeth Peabody, the movement had roots in Boston. In 1877 Mrs. Quincy A. Shaw opened kindergartens around Boston, running them at her own expense. By 1886 there were twenty in and near Boston, serving about thirteen hundred poor children, all supported by Mrs. Shaw.

Organizations came into being and disappeared quickly, as new things were tried and taken up or failed for lack of interest or funds. Everything was tried—fresh air, free nursing, free clothing, free milk, and instruction on nutrition. The child seemed to be the center of the city.[53]

One reform centered on the need for young people to learn to do something with their hands—a simple dissatisfaction with a school curriculum which emphasized classical subjects while ignoring learning through manipulative skills. The work of Victor Della Vos had been exhibited at the Philadelphia Centennial Exposition in 1876 and greatly influenced American educators to an incorporation of the mechanical skills and manual training in the schools. Some of these programs emphasized mere manipulation (clay modeling, for instance); there was no practical or vocational objective. The training, it was thought, would be a good in itself and would keep the boys from crime. "Manual training is corrective and uplifting." It counteracted the effects of the streets, gangs, and the normal destructiveness of boys. "It is the enemy of indifference and willfulness, because every step requires self-

control, thoughtfulness, care." To its friends, manual training was a near perfect therapy; "the boy's wood and tools are
realities; they register his temper; he must be sincere with
them, for his work stands plainly visible, approving or con-
demning him."[54]

Reflecting much of the same interest but having a more
specific objective were those who worked for vocational and
industrial training. While responding to the special needs of
an industrial age, occasionally, however, advocates of trades
schools directed their fire against labor unions, seeing industrial training as a means of breaking the union's monopoly
of skill.[55] Most often, however, the reformers merely recognized the importance of skills and wanted to provide the
means of training the poor. The apprentice system was in
the past, it was noted, and while few wished to return to the
harshness of that system,[56] the need for some method of im-
parting skills to the young was considered urgent. The large
mass of unskilled labor increased the problems of unemployment during hard times; the low wages that unskilled labor
drew made the unemployed's plight more miserable.[57] Negro
and Indian examples of trades schools were used to show that
even the lowest could be trained.[58] As it was, the Children's
Aid Society reported, boys and girls had little opportunity to
learn a trade. They drifted from job to job, gaining experience at nothing. They "make no progress from year to year,
and upon arriving at manhood and womanhood find themselves unskilled in any kind of labor, and unable to earn such
wages as will make a high standard of living possible."[59]

This anxiety about vocational training opportunities was
compounded by other senses of urgency. There was a need
for compulsory education, a need for control of juvenile
crime, a need to teach girls domestic trades, a need to accul-
turate immigrant families. Some ladies expressed concern over
the surrender of womanly virtues in an industrial world.[60]

The result of all this concern was the almost spontaneous

eruption of trades schools endowed by private funds.[61] But, in addition, some private individuals, notably Mrs. Augustus Hemenway, began to set up classes in sewing, cooking, carpentry, printing, and so on, in the public schools. These classes were maintained by private funds until they proved workable; then the city took them over.[62]

This emphasis on industrial training is further evidence of the highly pragmatic inclination of the charity reformers. Their efforts were directed to meet some present and observable need, rather than to work toward some abstract principle or goal; no discussions of child-labor reform are to be found in the literature.[63] The reformers thought of themselves as facing the hard, industrial realities. It may be argued that, despite their astringency of view, they overlooked obvious things—a mass of unskilled labor was important to the industrial society that they welcomed. Yet they clearly saw the need of training. And they were even willing to challenge some cherished myths. Contrary to the myth, they knew that a boy who worked as a telegraph messenger was, as an adult, best prepared to be a telegraph messenger, not the president of the company.

Much then fell to the public schools. James R. Reynolds, of the New York Associated Charities, told a meeting of the Associated Charities that the public schools were failing to meet their challenge. The schools tended to achieve nothing but mental training, he said, when at least fifty percent of the children educated in public schools would earn their livelihoods by their hands. "In the mental development of the child he uses his hands as the instrument of his mind and the development of both should advance with equal pace." "I am tired," Reynolds complained, "of being visited by children graduating from our public schools but not able to do anything."[64] The schools, too, in the end were asked to meet the real need of the child, to train what in a later year would be called the whole child.

NOTES

1. Henry W. Thurston, *The Dependent Child* (New York, 1930)—see Chs. 3, 4, and p. 40; Charles Loring Brace, *The Best Method of Disposing of Our Pauper and Vagrant Children* (New York, 1859), 3. Public institutions make criminals out of children in their care.

2. Boston Society for the Care of Girls, *One Hundred Years of Work in Boston* (Boston, 1919), passim—the Female Asylum, before name changed in 1909. Change in methods ("Records," October 1901); change apprentice system (October 1902); changes in indenture (April 1906); change program (December 1909). Manuscript records among papers of the Boston Children's Aid Association.

3. Children's Friend Society, *Reports:* history and purpose (XXXVI [1869], 3; XLVIII [1881], 5–6); considers change (XXXVII [1870], 5–6). The Society hereinafter cited as CFS.

4. Boston Asylum and Farm School, *Report*, XLVIII (1883), 1–3, 5.

5. CFS, *Report*, XLIII (1876), 7; XLV (1878), 5, 7; L (1883), 11–12; LXII (1895), 6; LXIII (1896), 29; LXIV (1897), 8.

6. Female Asylum, "Records," May 1890, July 1892, June and July 1893, June 1900, April 1901, August 1903. The names of the children and parents are not mentioned at the request of the Boston Children's Aid Association.

7. CFS, *Report* L (1883), 11; LX (1893), 12; LXII (1895), 7.

8. Female Asylum, "Records," October 1889; SPP, *Report*, XXXIII (1868), 6.

9. CFS, *Report*, XL (1873), 5; Female Asylum, "Records," August 1893. January 1895, October and November 1899.

10. "Orphan Children," *Lend A Hand*, I (June 1886), 317.

11. Female Asylum, "Records," October 1890, January 1895.

12. CFS, *Report*, XXXVII (1870), 6; Female Asylum, "Records," May 1893, August and September 1894.

13. Female Asylum, "Records," March 1901, November and December 1891, January and November 1893, July 1894; July 1889, refusal to interfere.

14. Ibid., April 1906 (see also May, June, and October 1906); August 1901 (see also January, February, March, June, July, September 1901, and May 1902); more problems of feeble-minded (December 1892, March 1902, August and September 1897).

15. Boston Female Asylum, *Reminiscences of the Boston Female Orphan Asylum* (Boston, 1844); Thurston, *Dependent Child*, 57–58.

16. Female Asylum, "Records," December 1896, January and August 1897.

17. Ibid., October and November 1890, January 1891, August and September 1892.

18. Ibid., August and September 1891, March 1910.

19. Ibid., March and April 1906, November 1890, January, April, May, September 1891.

20. CFS, *Report*, XLV (1878), 6–7.

21. Lying-In, *Report* (1887), 7–8.

22. CFS, *Report*, XLIV (1877), 4–5.

23. Instructive District Nurses, "Records of meetings of the Board of Directors," March 25, 1891. These manuscript records are among the papers of the Boston Visiting Nurses Association.

24. CFS, *Report*, LXVII (1900), 5.

25. Henrietta L. Synot, "Institutions and Their Inmates," *Contemporary Review*, XXVI (1875), 488; CFS, *Report*, XLVII (1880), 8; contracting list, XXXVII (1870), 5; XLI (1874), 7; LV (1888), 13; LVII (1890), 8; Mrs. Josephine Shaw Lowell quoted from NCCC, *Proceedings* [1885], 465, also in *Lend A Hand*, I (July 1886), 390; I (June 1886), 253.

26. Annie Adams Fields discovered the cottage plan in 1876 at a breakfast with Governor Bagley of Michigan. She says, "he gave us a detailed account of his school on the cottage plan for the children formerly shut up in poor houses and public institutions. He says it is a kind of purgatory between the hell of the institution or gutter and the heaven of adoption. He does not mean to have the children retained there, but only educated in passing into some good home. We were deeply touched by his story of scenes he had witnessed and the work he had tried to perform" (Diary, September 26, 1876).

27. CAS, *Report*, XXI (1885), 14; see also VIII (1872), 5–6.

28. Robert Treat Paine, "Address delivered March 24, 1890," among the papers of the Children's Aid Association.

29. CAS, *Report*, VIII (1872), 5–6.

30. Ibid., IX (1873), 6; see comment on girls' home (VII [1871], 7; CAS, "Visitors' Records," June 7, 1872, and January 1, 1873).

31. CAS, *Report*, IX (1873), 4.

32. Ibid., XIX (1883), 4; XX (1884), 4–5.

33. Children's Mission to the Children of the Destitute, *Annual Report* (1850), 9–10. The Associated Charities approved ("Records," December 8, 1899); newsboys without licenses were to be arrested as beggars.

34. "Saving Boys and Girls," Boston *Evening Transcript*, January 17, 1891; CAS, *Report*, XXI (1885), 15, is first to distinguish between simple oversight and probation; see also Society's "Bureau of Information Records," November 4, 1908; CAS, "Visitors' Records," January 30, 1869, February 3, 1892, and January 4, 1893.

35. CAS, "Visitors' Records," July 19, 1870; CAS, *Report*, XXVI (1890); Paine, "Address, delivered March 24, 1890"; Reverend Charles G. Ames, "Address," among the papers of the Children's Service Association.

36. CAS, "Visitor's Records," January 1871, for an especially question-

ing report; March 1883, October 1870, January 1867; CAS, *Report,* XXII (1886), 6–7.

37. CAS, "Visitors' Records," April 5, 1883, March 4, 1886, July 3, 1867, May 14, 1868, and May 3, 1867; November 3, 1883; April 5, 1867, and March 6, 1868; CAS, "Pine Farm Committee Report," May 2 and June 4, 1894, and see also CAS, *Report* XIX (1883), 8–9.

38. CAS, "Visitors' Records," July 16 and August 27, 1873; CAS, *Report,* XIX (1883), 4.

39. CAS, *Report,* XIX (1883), 4.

40. Ibid., II (1866), 7–8; Massachusetts State Board of Charities, *Report* (1868), lxviii.

41. CAS, *Report,* III (1867), 4; Massachusetts State Board of Charities, *Report* (1867), lxix: the "small sum paid for the board of a child for a short time would cost the state less than his support in the institution, and would often secure good treatment in a good family," is concluded from a study initiated by the Board.

42. CAS, *Report,* XV (1879), 8; XX (1884), 6.

43. Ibid., XXII (1886), 8–9.

44. Ibid., 9; and also 8–11.

45. Ibid., XXV (1889), 14, is where the quote occurs; almost every report, however, carried some statement about these libraries. It is interesting to note that in adjusting to changing needs the CAS transformed the committees responsible for this work into managers of group work with children. These committees presently utilize the techniques of group therapy. (From an interview with Miss Marjory C. Warren of the Boston Children's Aid Association.)

46. Ibid., XXIII (1887), 11–12.

47. Ibid., 11–13; XXVI (1890), 5.

48. Ibid., XXIV (1888), 16; XXVI (1890), 5.

49. See dissertation copy of this study (on file in Harvard University, Archives), Appendix A, for sample of CAS case records for 1899.

50. CAS, "Visitors' Records," December 1880, which questions Mr. Washburn's authority.

51. CAS, *Report,* XXVII (1891), 10–13; XXIX (1893), 10.

52. Phillips Brooks, "Address before the Children's Aid Society, March 24, 1890," among papers of Children's Service Association.

53. Julia A. Ames, "The Crèche, or Baby Mission," *Lend A Hand, I* (October 1886), 736–739; Constance MacKenzie, "Free Kindergartens," *Lend A Hand, I* (August 1886), 603–606; Woods, *City,* 71–72.

54. Woods, *City,* 238. Most organizations that worked with children would make some effort to include this training (CAS, "Pine Farm Committee Report," January 1, 1894); Lawrence Cremin, *Transformation of the School* (New York, 1961), 22–24.

55. SPP, *Report,* XXXIV (1869), 15–16.

56. Letter from Edward E. Hale to Thomas W. Higginson, December 4, 1887, Hale papers, Houghton.

57. CAS, *Report,* XXVII (1891), 25.

58. IAS, *Report,* XLV (1880), 13–14.

59. CAS, *Report,* XXVII (1891), 25. There was general agreement that trades schools were needed: IAS, XLVI (1881), 7–8; CAS, *Report,* XXVI (1890), 13, and XXVII (1891), 24–25: Boston *Evening Transcript,* January 17, 1891; Woods, *City,* 231–244; *Lend A Hand,* I (February 1886), 22–101, (July) 442–446.

60. Fields, Diary, December 13, 1871; three women met to discuss the best allocation of state funds for a women's university.

61. The Boston Industrial School for Girls (Domestics) had been established in 1853 but made changes in 1880 *(Lend A Hand* I [July 1886], 444); North Bennet St. Industrial School was established in 1881; South End Industrial School (Norfolk House Centre), 1884; Industrial Home for Crippled and Deformed Children, 1893—to name only a few.

62. *Lend A Hand* carried a regular report by Lucretia P. Hale "Walks in Boston Public Schools," which discusses this matter fully.

63. *Lend A Hand,* I (May 1886), 305, is a rare discussion of the problem of child labor; it is a report of the New York Women's Conference.

64. James R. Reynolds (New York Associated Charities), "Address before the Boston Associated Charities, November 8, 1900"; a typescript of this address is among the papers of the Family Service Association.

5

The Emergence of
a Profession

SINCE charity reform demanded diversification and greater precision of program, it followed that the volunteer would have to give way to the expert. So it was in the Children's Aid Society. Charles W. Birtwell, as soon as he was able, divided the Society's program into bureaus, in charge of which he placed paid agents. By 1890, the Society employed two staff persons in the Bureau of Information, three in the Placing-out Agency, one to deal with probation and "graduates," a woman to supervise the home libraries, and a bookkeeper. In time, the staff would direct the whole operation, committees from the Board merely hearing their reports. After all, the paid agents were experts; the committees merely carried their recommendations to the Board meetings.

Other societies bent on reform developed similarly, establishing trends which profoundly affected the character of charity work with the poor. There was growing bureaucratization or centralization—reliance on an administrator. There was an increasing demand for trained personnel—those choosing charity work as a vocation. And, consequently, there was a deemphasis of volunteerism. These developments were manifested to different degrees in the various charitable societies and some did not change at all.

The Industrial Aid Society, for instance, was centralized almost from the beginning. Specializing in the service of finding work for the unemployed, it needed no institution or visitors. It maintained an office and a small paid staff. Unlike the Children's Aid Society, the Industrial Aid's Board of Managers kept a tight rein over the staff, and, at least until 1900, retained leadership in policy determination. The staff's work was defined in 1886. The Agent had charge of the men's and boys' departments, keeping a register of applicants, available jobs, a record of advertisements, and making quarterly and annual statements to the Board of Managers. He had an assistant in the male department who worked outside the office, negotiating with employers in and out of Boston. The assistant tried to find employment for applicants, dispatched them to their destinations and organized gangs of men for temporary jobs. Another assistant was to "have the charge of the female department and as far as possible to obtain information as to the character of applicants by personal visits and by investigation."[1]

At the first quarterly meeting of 1890, the Board of Managers discussed the inefficiency of the Central Office, referring the matter to the Executive Committee. Considering no half-way measures, the Executive Committee recommended the discharge of the staff and the employment of a new General Agent at a salary of $1440 per year. The new Agent's duties were the same, but he was under the supervision of a yearly appointed three-man committee. The Agent was permitted assistants in the male and female departments at salaries of $804 and $504 per year, respectively. This yearly aggregate of $2748 was estimated to save the Society $452 annually. That this change was not a simple matter of economy is suggested by the fact that the Executive Committee spent the money in advertising.[2]

The Board of Directors accepted the Executive Committee's recommendations with the exception of those on salaries, Robert Treat Paine initiated the motion that appointed Mr. Henry Peterson General Agent at a salary of $1,500. He was allowed the two assistants, but the woman's salary was increased to $600. Except for an instance two years later when the assistant for the female department was asked to resign, there was no further trouble with the staff. Indeed, Mr. Peterson seemed to assume, in time, the stature of an executive officer of the Society. His reports to the Board showed initiative and leadership. Of course, as Robert Treat Paine's choice, he was in harmony with the new methods in charity.[3]

The Boston Provident Association began its process of change earlier than the other societies, but the transition is harder to pinpoint. One is conscious that in 1900 the Provident was centralized, bureaucratic, and forcefully led by a paid executive. Yet, there had been no single event—a hiring or firing or reshuffling—that could mark the innovation. As early as 1879 the Boston *Evening Transcript,* in a laudatory article claimed that the Provident was a "perfectly systematic charity." The effort to create a better system had begun two years earlier.[4]

Apparently dissatisfied with the performance of the voluntary visitors during the recent depression, the Association had made several efforts to reform. It already hired visitors, experienced with the Overseers of the Poor, to replace volunteers in a few districts. At the Board meeting in February 1877, Mr. Henry F. Jenks moved to have the work systematized "in the Central Office with a view to have more relief given there, and the labors of the visitors somewhat lessened." The discussion on the motion included comments on outdoor relief and Mr. Jenks's recommendation that male heads of families, where feasible, be required to apply for family relief, and that permanent cases be aided only at the Central Office. There was a coolness in response to the motion, but it was passed, including an amendment to increase the office staff if necessary. At the April meeting, the plan being in effect a month, the Board granted to Mr. Edward Frothingham, the new General Agent, permission to omit visitors' addresses from the *Directory* so that "all applications may be sent to the Central Office and thence distributed to visitors."[5]

Thus began a policy which was to bring into the Central Office the whole intelligence and administration of the Association. Most knowledge about the operation formerly had come from the visitors. They had been autonomous. With the new policy, however, instead of the visitors "helping . . . whomsoever they might fall in with who seemed to be worthy. . . . Visitors are now required to refer to the Central Office those who are strangers to them." The hope was to maintain greater control over the distribution of relief. In the Central Office the cases were "first looked up, and afterwards referred to the Visitor, if advisable." The Association was very pleased with the results of its experiment. "This *Centralization,* as it may be called, while it has increased our facilities for advantageously aiding the poor, has, at the same time, helped to promote economy."[6]

This kind of economy, however, was hard to explain to a public that might expect a small salary expenditure in an efficient charitable society's budget. The new administration cost money, if not in the Central Office itself, then because of the greater reliance on paid workers. In a city the size of Boston, they claimed, proper uplift required "unremitting application, patience, method, tact, and these are not to be had for nothing." Any amount of money which would save the ordinary needy in Boston from becoming "beggars and paupers, and as such preying upon the community" would be well spent. And again, four years later, the Association argued that since 1877 a new kind of economy had to be accepted, one that was willing to spend money to insure that "little or nothing is wasted on imposters or the unworthy." In the period since 1877 "not only has pauperism and street beggary steadily diminished, but the poor population of the city are far better cared for today than they were in 1876-77."[7]

A. C. Goodwin had been General Agent in those years before 1877. His resignation was natural enough; he was an old man. Yet one detects a new order in executive management after Goodwin's resignation. Goodwin had never exerted much influence on the Board. He wrote occasional reports, but his name was usually linked with a committee. In the Board records Goodwin is little in evidence. Instead, the president, Robert C. Winthrop, directed the meetings and discussion, often taking independent action; he was almost always supported.

The rest of the Board, in these early years, eagerly discussed new ideas. Often some member would bring up a private scheme to help cure a particular ill. Mr. Wadsworth, for instance, did not hesitate to suggest that the members think about new schemes for the employment of the poor. He had no specific plan, but thought "one might be matured by which the poor could be employed to improve their own dwellings." All such ideas were discussed fully. Most, like this one, were too vague and were "laid over for further discussion." But while Winthrop was president, it was the Board and Winthrop himself who dominated discussion.[8]

Edward Frothingham had been a member of the Board of Directors long before he took Goodwin's place. Frothingham became the auditor and a member of the Executive Committee in 1876, and in 1877 he was made General Agent. There was nothing striking about the change. But after Winthrop's retirement in 1879, Frothingham's reports came to dominate the Annual Reports. Indeed, Charles R. Codman, Winthrop's successor, was often absent from the meetings. In a short time the minutes of the Board consisted almost exclusively of the General Agent's report. It was a subtle change.

In the later years one is startled by a sudden question from a member of the Board. Mr. George A. James, who had

other problems with Mr. Frothingham, asked that the agent
specify an item in his statistical report called "special charities." "The General Agent explained the special charities of
the past month and said that he would be glad at any and
at all times to give full information on the subject and would
like to have members of the Board inquire into the subject."[9]

Mr. James had suggested in March 1892 that meal tickets
might be issued to parties importuning on the streets, "such
tickets to be good for a meal by special arrangement with
some respectable restaurant." James told of his personal experience with tickets he had managed at his own expense.
After a short discussion the matter was referred to Executive
Committee. It might well have died there had Mr. James not
been persistent. He was, at last, asked to attend the Executive
Committee and explain his plan further. Yet it was not until
the January 12, 1893, meeting of the Board that Mr. Grew
reported that "the Committee, after a thorough, unprejudiced
and careful examination and consideration of the whole matter, was unanimously of the opinion that it is not expedient
for the Boston Provident Association, as an Association, to
issue Meal Tickets." The fact is, however, that the Executive
Committee heard Mr. James at a meeting on November 2,
1892. After James left the room "the matter was discussed &
Mr. Frothingham was requested to collect information on the
subject & to report to the next meeting." If the Committee
gave the subject any further, careful consideration, it was
never recorded.[10]

There is ample evidence of Mr. Frothingham's initiative.
When William P. Fowler of the Overseers of the Poor wrote to
the Association requesting a special fund for widows and
orphans, it was Agent Frothingham, and not president Codman, who responded. Or, when Roxbury and Dorchester
appealed for help (they were outside the Association's limits),
"the whole matter was left with Mr. Frothingham to arrange
as he should deem best." And, in the new century, after the

usual report of the General Agent, the secretary could write: "After an informal talk on the advisability of getting younger men interested in the Association with a view of their joining the Board of Managers, but without taking any definite action thereon the meeting was dissolved."[11]

By no means all of Boston's charitable societies made similar changes in organization and staff. Some showed staunch resistance to change. Generally, the organizations which resisted change were those with limited, strictly defined objectives and those which were institutional. The Howard Benevolent Society, and the Fatherless and Widows Society, both restricted their aid to "Americans" who had seen better times. Neither permitted much change; they were pleased with their conservatism. The Fatherless and Widows Society, for instance, proudly qualified to receive money from a grant left by Augustus Hemenway which excluded charitable societies whose staffs were paid. It was so unassertive that its greatest concern was that it might be ignored. "With no paid officers and with no office, it is perhaps sometimes lost sight of in the midst of many other societies which come so much more actively to the front."[12]

Organizations which kept inmates tended against reform. Thus, the Boston Home for Aged Men, the Home for Aged Women, and the Home for Aged Colored Women maintained their simple staff arrangements of matrons, or superintendents responsible to a Board of Directors, and a visiting committee. Those asylums that did change, did so quite late.[13]

Reform in organization and staff were closely tied to the adoption of modern methods and deinstitutionalization. The Children's Friends Society spent some time discussing the feasibility of adopting a placing-out system before inviting Charles Birtwell to talk to them. Birtwell not only told them about new methods of child care, but he also recommended that they hire Sherman C. Kingsley. The Board appointed Kingsley its first General Secretary and abandoned its asylum.

Similarly, the Female Asylum discussed new methods in 1901. It began some placing out, while keeping the asylum. Mr. Birtwell shared his office with the Asylum's Mrs. Holmes, teaching her the methods of a visitor. It was not until 1908, however, that the Female Asylum converted fully to a placing-out system. At the suggestion of Zilpha Smith, Miss Mabelle B. Blake, of the Roxbury Associated Charities, was hired as the first agent of the Female Asylum.[14]

The increasing reliance, during the last decades of the century, on paid staff points up one of the most interesting paradoxes of the charity reform movement. The reform charities, especially the charity organization societies, placed great emphasis on the role of the volunteer. Yet in all organizations, especially the reforming ones, paid workers increased in number and importance from the 1870s on. Indeed, the practices of the Associated Charities, the Provident Association, and the Industrial Aid Society suggest that these Boston agencies were aiming for professional staffs earlier than is generally thought.[15]

The paradox was built into the very nature of Christian charity as a social movement. An attitude that found virtue in the act of benevolence and service—the giver was twice-blessed—was not consistent with one that insisted upon reform, social betterment, and uplift. The language of one was that of sympathy, describing both the giver and the receiver responding in unison to a single human condition. The language of the other was that of efficiency, denoting the knowledge that could prescribe the precise tool to effect a social as well as moral improvement. While one anticipated the callousness of the paid worker, suspecting anyone who would benefit from human misery, the other denigrated the well-meant fumbling of amateurs, subsuming them under the pejorative title, "Lady Bountiful." The charity reformers seemed to want to speak both tongues; here was the nub of the paradox.[16]

The Associated Charities tried from the beginning to re-
solve the paradox by separating two elements within the
organization. They allowed the voluntary visitors their prov-
ince of aid without alms, while the paid visitor distributed
relief. Each conference of the Associated Charities had, along
with its volunteers, one paid agent who offered counsel and
actually directed the conference's operations. The paid agents,
according to Robert Treat Paine, "must become, if only after
long study and patient practice and many failures, experts
in the art of helping struggling families permanently upward,
as well as experts in making a diagnosis of the causes of the
need."[17]

As it worked out, the volunteer had very little of the work
to do. Paine gave as an example of distribution of work Ward
10. The total number of cases registered at the Central Office
from this ward during the year 1879 to 1880 was 206. Some
were privately aided, leaving 103 cases. The paid agent found
many of these to be aged people needing only relief. Some
he found to be able to help themselves. Others were frauds
whom he exposed. Thus, only thirty-five cases, or one-third,
were decided in conference to be given to visitors. Of these,
the visitors could help only twenty-eight. The paid agent took
the brunt of the work.[18]

The urge of the volunteer persisted into the new century.
Part of this insistence was a kind of curiosity. Some women
in a college settlement in Boston asked the Instructive District
Nurses that some of "the ladies . . . be allowed to visit with
the nurses in order to see the poor more intimately in their
homes." They were refused.[19] A major reason, however, was
the belief that the volunteer had a potential for sympathy
that could not be trained or bought; the act of volunteering
was an act of compassion. The real gain was to be found in
the meeting of two worlds: "the mutual understanding, the
breadth of outlook, the changed point of view, the sympathy
. . . and finally the resulting modification of the ultimate

social factor, public opinion enlightened by facts, is a triumph."[20] The volunteer could not be abandoned despite the recognized need for efficiency.

The confusion of this duality is illustrated by a letter of Charles R. Codman to F. A. Bradford concerning Bradford's interest in membership on the State Board of Lunacy and Charity. Codman's Provident Association had for many years been committed to paid workers, yet Codman still looked for selfless experts. He told Bradford that the position brought no pay; indeed, it required a great deal of time and personal sacrifice and could not be considered political or in any other way self-serving. Bradford had to show his qualifications. Codman insisted on not only good character and reputation but also some special fitness for the job: "some experience in dealing with charitable institutions as well as experience in dealing with matters of general business." Thus, the candidate had to bring some expertness to the office. But, Codman went on, "you ought also to be able to show that you can give the time requisite & necessary for the proper performance of its duties."[21]

On the other hand, there was the early view that public charity should not be left to whim, but that the official should be paid and able. The Society for the Prevention of Pauperism asked if it was not wise to have a board or commission of officials or experts in care of the poor. Such a group, the Society suggested, would be "in receipt of salaries that would justify and require their entire devotion to this most serious branch of civic economics." Such men would soon save more than their salaries, it was assured. "But that would be a trifling gain compared with the variety, extent, and character of the good that they would secure . . . both for the poor and for the whole community."[22] But it was the anticipated economy of paid visitors which first appealed to organizations.

The Boston Provident Association first met the problem of paid visitors in 1853. The Association in its expansion into southern districts of the city merged with the South End Provident Association in 1852. The SEPA had used paid visitors, and the merged districts proposed to continue this practice. The Provident's managers wondered whether paid agents were in keeping with the practices of the Association. For the time, the matter was left unresolved.[23]

Under the pressure of the depression of 1873, however, the Provident Association, as an economy move, hired visitors who had had experience with the Overseers of the Poor. The results were gratifying. By 1875 the Association reported that the amount expended for fuel and provisions had been reduced by $2,024.67 over the previous year. "This decrease is partly owing to the employment of skilled Visitors in some of the worst sections of the city." Through their familiarity with the condition and needs of the poor, "and their skill in detecting cases of imposture," these visitors had been able to save money. Nor was this saving at the expense of any worthy case. Rather, it was money normally wasted upon the "idle and dissolute, who too frequently contrive to secure the material aid intended for the deserving poor."[24]

The real waste of charitable resources, and therefore the real damage to the poor, came from untrained volunteers. The Association claimed that the volunteer was often too soft and seldom able to distinguish real from fraudulent need. Furthermore, it "is well known that the kind-heartedness and sympathy of a Visitor often increases the number of applicants for help." Thus volunteerism worked against the aims of the Association. Increased almsgiving, after all, merely meant increased begging. "The object of the Association has always been to prevent begging and pauperism by timely aid, and not to support those who live principally by begging." And, of course, a big problem with volunteers was that they were undependable. Under the pressure of crisis, many of them resigned.[25] These arguments were continually reiterated in the Association's published reports.

In 1882 the Association did give the volunteers credit, but still ambivalence persisted. The Society claimed that it could not operate successfully without a corps of volunteers. It was true that money was wasted and mistakes were made, but volunteers added something. "Their enthusiasm gives vitality to the Association," it was claimed. Because there were these amateurs there was "less danger of falling into the routine of an official way of doing business,—by which we mean a habit of looking upon all applicants as so many cases to be put through a certain given form of relief."[26]

Excluding such occasional slight praise to the volunteer, the Association was committed to the paid agent. And they were ready to defend the inevitable rising costs. A Boston newspaper criticized the increased expense of charity at the Provident Association, noting that "it has crept up from 33 per cent in 1881 to 42 per cent in 1885; and that, while it cost sixty-two cents to distribute a dollar in the former year, it required nearly seventy-five cents for the same purpose in the latter." Edward Frothingham merely pointed out that the purpose of the Society was suppression of pauperism and beggary, not almsgiving, that far too much had been given in 1874 and 1875. The estimate of the Association should be in its reduction of almsgiving, not in the ease of it. And in a later year, Edward Frothingham could remember that "Captain Goodwin once said . . . that his Visitors gave him more trouble than the applicants." He was relieved to report that there "is none of the friction, vexation, uncertainty, delay, and waste, inseparable from a system of universal volunteer visiting for the relief of the indigent." To the Provident, at least, the paid visitor was a savior. One could be more certain of standards when a "trained" man was hired.[27]

F. C. Cowing received his training, as did most of the Provident visitors in these years, through his experience with the Overseers of the Poor. He came to the Boston Provident in 1884 and took up the work in South Boston. His methods were not difficult to understand. The Association considered him a strict disciplinarian. "He holds fast to the rule (the only safe one in dealing with a certain class of applicants) which decides that a family had better not receive help if by any possibility it can be made to get along without it." His effort was to determine whether a family, through its relatives, friends, or by its own exertions, was capable of self-support; failing in these resources the family was deserving of help. Cowing's "peculiar aptness" for handling problems of the poor was that he "holds tenaciously to the principle that the best way to help the poor is by teaching them to help themselves, and sometimes a little hardship is better than help." Widely known in South Boston, he used his contacts as intelligence sources. He had limitless ways of determining whether or not a man drank or had other bad habits and whether there were undisclosed resources. Through "constant vigilance" he was able to determine actual conditions and detect deceptions. By such methods Cowing, and others like him, were able to reduce the relief roles of the Provident Association. Despite his previous training and fourteen years' experience with the Provident, the Association remembered him, on his death, not for new techniques or methods but for "his judicious keeping down of the expenses in that section."[28]

To the Provident, a paid visitor was a trained visitor, and training was experience that would steel one to say no to a sad story. Indeed, until the last decade of the century, there was no training in any specific art that charitable organizations would demand. Only as far as nurses' and doctors' work among the poor can be considered charity, were there skilled workers. The Instructive District Nurses went among the poor, aided them and taught simple techniques of self-help and hygiene. The doctors of the Boston Dispensary gave free care and got training in return. The nurses were often quite effective as social workers. They were trained not only in their skill but trained to teach the poor in order to preserve the good results of free medicine.[29]

But there was no training available to the charity workers in the 1870s and 1880s. When an organization hired a person, it based its judgment on references. When the Female Asylum considered a new matron in 1889 it found itself with four applicants. Annie M. K. Treat was a widow, forty-seven years old and a native of Frankfort, Maine. She "has had a varied experience—has had two years in hospitals." Miss Homans, the private secretary to Mrs. Augustus Hemenway, "spoke highly of her and said that she had a great faculty of making a household harmonious." Miss Bellows of the Homeopathic Hospital gave a similar report. The second applicant, Miss Hunt, was forty and had had charge of a cottage in an institution in Davenport, Iowa. "Her references were good. She is fond of children, conscientious & religious, but there was no testimonial with regard to her judgment. She had had but little experience in house keeping." Mrs. Alice Neale, on the other hand, had held a similar position in a New York asylum but left when the administration changed. Finally, Mrs. Madison had been ten years a matron of a training school for nurses, and had been a matron of the Home for Aged Women in Providence, Rhode Island. The Board of Directors, clearly influenced by references of known people, took Mrs. Treat for a two-month trial.[30]

Lacking objective criteria for expertness, societies relied on experience in similar organizations or on the word of trusted people. This made for a fuzziness of definition that everywhere characterized the work. Even *Lend A Hand* magazine noted the problem. Edward Everett Hale cautioned Zilpha D. Smith that at first the magazine's pages would be filled with "a good deal of elementary talk." But he had confidence that in time the articles would become more precise, and he would print "what experts are glad to write and glad to know.''[31] But this had to wait for definition, control, and teaching: communication through the cooperation of societies and the creation of schools of social work.

The very thrust of charity reform—organization, and reliance on paid personnel—worked out informal methods for solving its chief problem. Greater cooperation between agencies—the sharing of intelligence—usually resulted in some statement of method. Even conflict, such as that between the Boston Provident and the Associated Charities, required each organization to define its procedures. Such definition was education. Each Conference of the Associated Charities was intended to be a seminar in which voluntary and paid visitors shared insights and experiences. The Executive Committee of the conference brought to it the pooled intelligence of the larger organization. Thus, ideally, the experience of the individual worker became the experience of the group. The Children's Aid Society's willingness to share its personnel with other agencies facilitated training, definition, and standardization of method. Informal gatherings such as the Monday Evening Club or various teas and luncheons, where social workers came together to discuss their work, gave them a greater sense of vocation than they could have had in 1870.[32]

By far the most important single force which made for cooperation and communication was the National Conference on Charities and Correction, which first met in 1874, following three years of successful conferences of the Michigan, Illinois, and Wisconsin Boards of Charities and Reform. The first meeting of the Conference was held with the American Social Science Association, but subsequent meetings were independent. There were only twenty people present and about four states represented in 1874.

The organization grew. The first conference betrayed a public bias in the topics it discussed: state boards of charities; care of the insane; public buildings; pauperism, settlement laws, outdoor relief, almshouses; city charities and the statistics of crime and pauperism. In one way or another these original topics remained part of the agenda, but new topics soon were added. In 1875 the states began to make individual reports and hold discussions on medical charities (including hospitals); care of dependent children, care of delinquent children, and immigration were added. They began to talk about tramps in 1877, prison reform (convict labor) in 1878, charity organization and epileptics in 1880, deaf and blind education in 1882, care of the feeble-minded in 1884, the Indian question in 1887, and women's work in philanthropy in 1891. Under these headings there was room to discuss the kindergarten movement, orphan asylums and children's homes, the placing-out system, probation, and interstate migrations. By 1900, the National Conferences on Charities and Correction still discussed state and, strictly speaking, public problems. Yet, items of general interest predominated: "Improvements in Medical Care for the Insane," "Some Recent Developments in Child-Saving," "Home-placing," "The Place of the Kindergarten in Child-Saving," "Development of the Individual," "Charity Organization Applied to Mission Work," and "Compulsory Education in its Relation to the Charity Problem."[33]

The conferences provided forums for both education and criticism. Matters were often hotly debated. Although seldom was there immediate resolution of conflict, contention was healthy for both the innovator and the conservative. For instance, the movement away from institutions and asylums (especially in child care) was pronounced in the Conference as an assault against institutions, as such. The attack brought heated defense.[34] The chairman mediated, and there grew out of this dispute (which never quite ended) a better definition of methods for both groups, a needed movement to reform institutional practices, and a general interest in the issues. And as a forum, the Conference brought together the most important names in social service. The Boston charity-organization leaders, Robert Treat Paine and Zilpha D. Smith, could meet with Charles S. Fairchild, Charles D. Kellogg, Professor Theodore Dwight, Louise Lee Schuyler, and Mrs. Josephine Shaw Lowell—all of New York—as well as Seth Low and George B. Buzelle of Brooklyn, James W. Walk of Philadelphia, and Mary Richmond of Baltimore. The Conference also made specialists available, such as experts in care for the insane and feeble-minded.

Besides giving broader perspective to the work, the Conference forced the practitioners to see their problems as something more than local. By 1900 the Conference was truly national with every state represented. The conferences had been held in almost every large city in the country. The significance of this national organization should not be underestimated. Not only did it give localities a sense of commonness with the rest of the country, but the field was broadened from which societies could draw their staff. When the Chicago Relief and Aid Society wanted an executive officer, it turned first to Charles W. Birtwell, offering him an attractive salary. The Children's Aid Society met its offer, however. The Chicago agency was then successful in hiring Sherman Kingsley from the Children's Friends Society. While this has the qualities of a raid, it shows, nonetheless, how in the early years of the twentieth century both organizations and staff were freer than they could have been in 1870.[35]

Massachusetts people participated in the conferences from the start. As one would suspect, Zilpha Smith, Charles Birtwell, and Sherman Kingsley gave much of their time. Robert Treat Paine was elected president in 1895. When the conference was held in Boston in 1881, of the 239 members present 53 were from Boston alone. By 1900, over 60 people from Boston were listed as members.[36]

This National Conference was not alone; there were local conferences. Although strictly a public agency, the State Board of Charities made an early effort to bring together community intelligence on matters of charity and public welfare. It published its reports from 1865 to 1869, which often went beyond narrowly defined interests of State institutions of the time. For instance, early assessments of the European attempts at decentralized care of children appear in these reports.[37] In 1892 the New England Conference on Charities, Corrections, and Philanthropy was organized in Lynn, Massachusetts. It covered the same ground as the National Conference, but it gave more intense consideration to local problems. The New England Conference was not an effort to compete with the national group. Rather, it shows the pervasiveness of the conference idea.[38]

Such conferences went far toward giving the charity worker a feeling of subculture and of membership in a profession.[39] They gave national scope and provided a reservoir of national experience. They publicized where experience was needed and where experienced workers could be found. But while they educated in a broad way, they could not develop a true discipline. The need for skilled workers persisted, and the conferences could not supply that need.

Recruitment and training remained a problem into the next century. Speaking before the Civic Club of Philadelphia in 1897 Miss Mary Richmond explored the problem of training; she presented a concrete proposal the same year at the National Conference on Charities and Correction. As late as June 1911, Charles Birtwell was to join Miss Richmond and Jane Addams in an appeal for the recruitment of workers.[40]

Mary Richmond remarked that talent was not enough. It could only "prepare the way for success, when special knowledge and training have been added." She applauded the on-the-job training programs instituted by some agencies. As good as such training was, however, it tended to a narrow specialization. What was needed was to place charitable work on the same level as the other professions. While this meant the rejection of claims of noble self-sacrifice, "in placing philanthropy on a level with the sciences of education, theology and medicine, we advance her true importance; for it becomes at once evident that, as a science, as a body of organized fact, she has lagged behind any of these." The true need, Miss Richmond claimed, was for a "Training School in Applied Philanthropy." The school Miss Richmond visualized would not demand quick specialization; theory and practice would go hand in hand. The school would be in a large city; the students could see how charitable organizations worked while they learned general principles.

The first school of applied philanthropy opened as a summer school in 1898. It featured practical work and a wide variety of lectures (for the 7 years of its existence the school had 145 faculty members). The students in 1900 paid a fee of ten dollars, heard lectures by Francis G. Peabody, Homer F. Folks, Robert de Forest, Edward T. Devine, Charles Birtwell, and Zilpha Smith. During the first three weeks of the course, the students studied the treatment of needy families in their own homes and heard thirteen addresses. They made several visits to the Lower East Side. The fourth week was devoted to the study of the care of dependent, neglected, and delinquent children, with six addresses. In the fifth week the students visited medical charities and institutions with addresses at some of them. And the last week was devoted to study of "constructive social movements" for neighborhood improvement. The Summer School continued for seven years with such a program. The establishment of the New York School of Philanthropy in 1904 gave a full-time course for college graduates who were interested in social work. The Summer School continued, but with a student body of predominantly experienced workers.[41]

In 1904, coincidental with the establishment of the New York School of Philanthropy, the Harvard-Simmons School for Social Workers was opened. Contributions were made to Harvard University stipulating its cooperation with Simmons

College. The first director was Jeffrey R. Brackett, Ph.D., former lecturer at Johns Hopkins University and President of the Board of Charities in Baltimore. Zilpha Smith was appointed Assistant Director. Dr. Brackett and Miss Smith gave lectures in their specialities. A four-year program for women leading to a bachelor's degree was adopted; three years of work in one of the other schools at Simmons College was demanded. It was not until 1914 that a definite list of courses was required. By 1913 only six degrees had been granted since most students took special courses and were not enrolled in a degree program. By 1916, when Harvard dropped its affiliation, over five hundred women had been registered but less than a dozen men. The Russell Sage Foundation gave the school $7,500 in 1907 for special research and fellowships; the grant was increased to $10,000 in 1908. This foundation continued its interest and aid in subsequent years. In 1916, a school of Simmons College, unattached and sporting a new name—The School of Social Work—proceeded to iron out the kinks in a training program for workers in a new profession.[42]

When Charles Birtwell spoke from the platform of Ford Hall in 1911, the recruitment of men for training in the profession had been a major problem. He found the seminaries failing to train men towards social responsibilities. Other professions would have their appeal, but social work, Birtwell thought, required a special kind of man. This man had to be drawn to the work by a special call. Agencies could not campaign by solicitation; rather there "should be a campaign of revelation," Birtwell exclaimed. Apparently, he anticipated attracting the young men whom the seminaries missed.[43]

Birtwell himself had been brought into charity work through Francis G. Peabody's course in social ethics at Harvard. With him were men like William Pear, Sherman C. Kingsley, and Homer Folks. They were, according to Professor Peabody, a group "which found in this new vocation a professional opportunity, ranking, as they believed, with the established professions of Law, Medicine or Divinity and they gave themselves to these studies with the same motives which, a generation earlier, would have prompted them to study for the Christian Ministry." Birtwell did not forsake his own experience. He turned to Harvard as a possible source for this new work. From 1894 until 1904 he served as Executive Director of the Social Service Committee of the Phillips Brooks House at Harvard. There he kept over one hundred men active every year in some kind of social work: visiting the poor, entertaining, teaching at the Prospect Union, and so on. By such means he hoped to make young men aware that a new profession existed—a new ministry—that demanded their service. And it was still a pioneering work. After all, Birtwell's occupation was still listed in 1925 (the last class report before his death) under the "miscellaneous" heading.[44]

The maturing of Boston's charities into Boston's social work occurred between 1870 and 1910. This development is marked by greater centralization and bureaucracy, the rise of the paid executive, the greater reliance on paid, trained staff, the definition through national and local conferences and, finally, the training in the arts of social work through professional schools. This change was significant not only for what it meant in the care of the poor, but also for the emergence of a new profession.

When Charles Birtwell joined the Children's Aid Society in 1885, it had been inconceivable that a person might train himself for a career in charitable work. Upon his resignation in 1911, however, the Children's Aid Society could reasonably expect to replace him with a man who had training and experience in a similar organization. J. Prentice Murphy had specialized in political science, history, economics, and sociology at the University of Pennsylvania. He had been a special investigator for the Pennsylvania Child

Labor Committee, a club director of the University Settlement, an agent for the Pennsylvania Society to Protect Children from Cruelty, an investigator into woman and child
labor in the canning factories in New York, a resident of the
East Side Settlement House in New York City; and, for
the three years before coming to the Children's Aid, Murphy
had been the superintendent of the Children's Bureau in
Philadelphia.[45]

Along with this growing sense of profession was the con-
comitant diminution of the importance of the Board of Directors. In the early years the Board defined the purpose of
the organization, raised funds to sustain it, formulated all
policy, and did much of the day-to-day work. As the professional grew in importance, however, the daily operations and
much policy was left in his hands; after all, he was the expert.
The Board members became inactive, as in the Boston Provident, or, as in the Children's Aid, advisory or consultant. Of
course, they kept their legal status; Board meetings were
required to change the rules, to budget funds, and to change
property holdings. Certainly the members, as influential people in the community, still made important official contacts,
and still raised funds. But their role became more and more
restricted to these matters.

One might expect some contention between the professional staff and the members of the Board as power was
shifted. But the first wave of professionals were not aliens
who arrived with a new ideology and a demand for authority.
Rather, they were people who might well have been members
of the Board themselves; sometimes they were. Zilpha Smith
was executive secretary in an organization which had been
committed from its inception to a professional staff. Born in
Pembroke, Massachusetts, to an old Massachusetts family
(both sides went back to the original settlement), Miss Smith
had Yankee roots. Her family was solid middle-class (her
father was a shipbuilder). Thus in social essentials, except

for wealth, she was little different from any other member of the Associated Charities' Board of Directors. Charles Birtwell came from a middling family in Lawrence, Massachusetts. Although he had to work his way, dropping out because of health, he graduated summa cum laude from Harvard College in 1885. Birtwell's continued work with Harvard students through the Phillips Brooks House permitted him to bridge a social gap between himself and members of his Board of Directors. Edward Frothingham was not only from an old, prominent Massachusetts family but he was a member of the Board of Directors of the Boston Provident Association before he became its General Secretary.[46]

Not that these new executives were of a particular social rank, but neither were they strangers to society. They were trusted people to whom it was natural to pass power. They were sensitive and respectful of the attitudes and feelings of the Board members. When Sherman C. Kingsley resigned from the Children's Friends Society (an organization which had been very slow in changing to new methods), the directors were moved to express "their admiration of the manner in which, soon after he became the general secretary, he made plans for enlarging the service to the children of the community, always showing respect for the good deeds previously accomplished by the Society and at the same time endeavoring to have the future life of the Society a period of greater usefulness."[47]

An interesting contrast is the short tenure of Dr. Stuart A. Queen as Director of Simmons's School of Social Work. A former Assistant Professor of Constructive Philanthropy at Goucher College and Educational Director of the American Red Cross, Dr. Queen was qualified for the position except that he was a non-Bostonian and unprepared for charitable organizations that were "chiefly in the hands of a circle of philanthropic workers recruited largely from Boston's conservative aristocracy." While Dr. Brackett had cooperated

with this group, "for socially he was one of them," Dr.
Queen was not only an outsider but he was also impatient.
Considered a "young man in a hurry," Dr. Queen ended two
uncomfortable years in Boston by taking a professorship at
the University of Kansas. Thus, conflict was more likely to
exist between insiders and outsiders than between professionals and Boards of Directors. The Boards were willing
enough, it seems, to give up absolute determination of policy, but not prestige and ultimate authority. So qualified, the
Boards were amenable to professionalization.[48]

By the end of the nineteenth century the word professional
rolled very easily off the tongues and pens of those who described workers in charitable organizations. Roy Lubove has
demonstrated that bureaucratization, specialization, training,
and occupational subculture—we have found them evident
as early as the 1850s in some organizations—gathered mo-
mentum so that by the mid-twentieth century they characterized the whole of the social work enterprise.[49] Some, then
and now, however, would hesitate calling social work a profession. Since any profession must, in some way, control itself
through administration or professional organization, have
practitioners who devote full working time to the calling,
define, perfect, and train its art or science, there is some justification in the frequent use of the term. By 1900, and surely
by 1910, evidence of these qualifications had appeared in
social work. The sociologist Bernard Barber would not quarrel about the name, except to qualify it as "marginal."[50] It
may have been only rudimentary, but professional intention
was clearly evident and there was strenuous effort to advance
its claim.

In 1915, Abraham Flexner, speaking before the National
Conferences on Charities and Correction, tried to determine
whether social work was the social aspect of already established professions. With some boldness before this audience,
Flexner concluded that social work did not qualify. It had

no unique purpose; thus it had no specific art or skill to teach. For once the social worker had isolated a problem, he had to turn to some established profession for treatment. "There is illness to be dealt with—the doctor is needed; ignorance requires the school; poverty calls for the legislator, organized charity, and so on."[51] Thus, using his absolutes, social work could only mediate between society and the established professions, never to reach the goal.

Absolutes mean little to us, however. The trends are well marked and significant. We know that charity cases were likely to be dealt with differently after, say, 1885 than they were earlier. And notably, in 1870, Mr. Flexner's question would not have been raised at all.

NOTES

1. IAS, "Executive Committee Minutes," October 20, 1886, 22–23. The manuscript records of the IAS, as well as the SPP, are to be found among the papers of the Boston Family Service Association.

2. IAS, "Report of the Managers' Quarterly Meeting," January 14, 1890; "Executive Committee," January 29, 1890, 26–27.

3. IAS, "Record of the Board of Directors," February 5, 1890; "Report of the Managers' Quarterly," January 20 and April 20, 1892; "Executive Committee," January 27, 1892; for Mr. Peterson's reports see IAS, *Reports*.

4. Often the way the staff is listed in the Annual *Reports* is the only concrete evidence of reorganization. See, however, the Boston *Evening Transcript*, November 3, 1879.

5. Provident, *Reports*, XXV (1876), 11, paid visitor is first mentioned; "Records," February 16, 1877, 28, and April 13, 1877, 32.

6. Provident, *Reports*, XXXI (1882), 8 and 9, author's emphasis.

7. Ibid., XXXVI (1887), 9–10; XL (1891), 7–8.

8. Provident, "Records," January 10 and February 14, 1879.

9. Ibid., April 14, 1892, 239.

10. Ibid., March 10, 1892, 238, and January 12, 1893, 247; also Provident, "Executive Committee Minutes," November 2, 1892.

11. Letter from William P. Fowler to the Boston Provident Association, February 23, 1899, and letter from Edward Frothingham to William P. Fowler, February 26, 1899 (copy); both letters are among the

papers of the Boston Family Service Association. Provident, "Records," March 14, 1899, 59; February 10, 1903, 96; and March 10, 1903, 97.

12. Fatherless and Widow's Society, *Report*, LXXXI (1898), 4, hereinafter cited as F&WS. A similar tone can be noted in the reports of the Howard Benevolent Society.

13. See Annual *Reports* of the Boston Home for Aged Men, Home for Aged Colored Women, the Boston Home for Aged Women, the CFS, and the manuscript records of the Female Asylum. The latter two organizations changed after 1900.

14. CFS, *Report*, LXVII (1900), 5 (and for Kingsley's connection with the CAS see above, note 8); loc. cit. and CFS, "Records," July and August 1900 (Kingsley's salary raised, May 1901); early suggestions to board out children were not warmly received by the Female Asylum ("Records," September 25, 1877).

15. Lubove, *Professional Altruist*, assumes that the change came late (Chs. 1, 2, 5).

16. Nothing illustrates this paradox more than *Lend A Hand* itself. Continually railing against indiscriminate, private giving and demanding an expert, scientific charity, it still found space for articles showing that women, because of their maternal inclinations, have a natural contribution to make to charity; they bind up the wounded, "but to the lasting helplessness and hurt of the wounded" (I [January 1886], 49); but the magazine also recognized the possible callousness of the professional (I [March 1886], 141–142).

17. Robert Treat Paine, "The Work of Volunteer Visitors of the Associated Charities Among the Poor; its Limitations, Allies, Number of Workers, Aims and Grand Results," an address given September 10, 1880, before the Social Science Conference (Saratoga, N.Y.) and printed as No. 17 of the Boston Associated Charities, *Publications* (n.p., n.d.), quoted p. 7.

18. Ibid., 9.

19. Instructive District Nurses, "Records of the Meetings of the Board of Directors," October 28, 1891. The papers of this organization are to be found in the offices of the Boston Visiting Nurses Association.

20. Elizabeth Peabody House, *Report*, VI (1901), 12.

21. Draft of a letter from Charles R. Codman to F. A. Bradford, March 2, 1891, Codman papers, MHS.

22. SPP, *Report*, XX (1855), 8–9.

23. Provident, "Records," October 25, 1852, and February 10, 1853.

24. Provident, *Report*, XXIV (1875), 8.

25. Ibid., XXV (1876), 9–10.

26. Ibid., XXXI (1882), 13.

27. Boston *Herald*, November 11, 1885; letter from Edward Frothingham to the Editors of the Boston *Herald*, November 13, 1885 (copy), among the papers of the Boston Family Service Association; Provident, *Report*, XXXVI (1887), 8.

28. Provident, *Report*, XXXVIII (1889), 11–12; "Records," January 11, 1898, 49.

29. Boston Dispensary, *Reports;* Instructive District Nurses, *Reports.* For a statement on the instructive character of the nurses' work, see their *Report*, VI (1892), 11.

30. Female Asylum, "Records," September 1889.

31. Letter from Edward Everett Hale to [Zilpha] Smith, January 8, 1886, Hale papers, MHS.

32. Paine, "The Work of Volunteer Visitors," 7–9; Charles Birtwell organized the Monday Evening Club of "paid officers of charities of Boston and vicinity" in 1893 (see Class of 1885, *Report*, V [1900]); informal meetings become very apparent in all of the records of these organizations. By 1909 the CFS had regular meetings of placing-out agents (CFS, "Records," February 1909); by 1910 the Female Asylum ("Records," September and November 1910). Before these years meetings were casual.

33. The following account is taken from NCCC, *Proceedings;* Frank J. Bruno, *Trends in Social Work, 1874–1956* (New York, 1957) gives a history of this Conference from 1874.

34. NCCC, *Proceedings* (1885), 459–467.

35. CAS, "Records," July 21 and November 2, 1903; letter from Sherman C. Kingsley to the Board of Directors, CFS, March 4, 1904 (copy), and CFS, "Records," May 1904, among the papers of Boston Children's Aid Association.

36. NCCC, *Proceedings* (1893), 10; see chart.

37. Massachusetts Board of State Charities, *Reports* (1865-69); Bruno, *Trends in Social Work*, Ch. 4.

38. *Lend A Hand*, while it existed, carried some report of local New England conferences; see, for instance, VIII (December 1894).

39. Lubove, *Professional Altruist*, Ch. 5; Bernard Barber, "Some Problems in the Sociology of Professions," in *The Professions in America*, ed. Kenneth S. Lynn (Cambridge, Mass., 1965), 22–24.

40. "The Training of Charity Workers" and "Need of a Training School in Applied Philanthropy," in *The Long View, Papers and Addresses by Mary Richmond*, ed. Joanna C. Colcord (New York, 1930), 86–98 and 99–104, resp. The latter article by Miss Richmond first appeared with critical comment by Miss Frances R. Morse of Boston in NCCC, *Proceedings* (1897), 181–188. Birtwell's comments are reported in the Boston *Herald*, June 12, 1911.

41. Elizabeth G. Meier, *A History of the New York School of Social Work* (New York, 1954), Chs. 1, 2, especially pp. 13–14.

42. Kenneth L. Mark, *Delayed By Fire: Being the Early History of Simmons College* (Concord, N.H., 1945), 121–125.

43. Boston *Herald*, June 12, 1911.

44. Francis G. Peabody makes special reference to Birtwell's participation in his social ethics course in a eulogy remembering Birtwell; a

copy is in the Harvard Archives, Class of 1885, "Charles W. Birtwell folder," memorial service given at Eliot Hall, Boston, June 2, 1932; details of Birtwell's work with the Phillips Brooks House in a newspaper clipping from the Springfield (Mass.) *Republican*, n.d., but in Birtwell's folder.

45. Boston *Transcript*, October 3 and 4, 1911; Boston *Record*, October 3, 1911. Clippings may be found in the folder cited in the preceding note.

46. Biographical information about Charles W. Birtwell may be found in Henry W. Thurston, *The Dependent Child* (New York, 1930), 161–201; Harvard College Class of 1885, *Class Reports*, Harvard University Archives (Widener Library); and the Boston *Herald*, May 21, 1932.

47. Quote on Kingsley from CFS, "Records," May 1904; for a short biography see Harvard University Archives, "Quinquinial File."

48. For biographical information regarding Zilpha D. Smith see Bruno, *Trends in Social Work*, 99–100; and I am indebted to Dr. Roy Lubove for sharing information with me that he uncovered for an article on Miss Smith to appear in the forthcoming *Notable American Women* (Radcliffe). For Frothingham see Provident, *Report*, LVI (1907); for comment on Dr. Queen see Mark, *Delayed By Fire*, 124.

49. Lubove, *Professional Altruist*.

50. Barber, "Some Problems."

51. Abraham Flexner, "Is Social Work a Profession?" in NCCC *Proceedings* (1915), 576–590; quote, 585.

6

Relief

THE depressions of 1873 and 1893 were crucial tests of the tradition of private relief of the poor. The benevolent societies which were the outgrowth of the reforms of the 1830s and 1840s were inadequate to handle increased demand for charity; population growth and intense industrial and economic distress combined to overburden existing agencies. Some people could remember the crisis of 1857, but few were prepared for these new depressions. The shocks were quite severe and long; the quick succession made the cumulative effect much greater than the mere sum of the two, for by the last decade of the century people had come to believe that depressions were normal and to be expected. In time, that would be the seed of discontent with a system which limited public relief and had no solution for emergencies other than ad hoc committees.[1]

During the crises, the ordinary distinctions between public and private relief tended to break down, as public offices were used to support relief activities financed through private subscription. Despite the confusion, however, there was still a conscious effort to distinguish the proper roles of the two types of relief agencies.

From the 1830s there had been an effort to place poor-relief under the control of responsible private individuals. Some reform energy had been directed against indiscriminate giving, but considerable pressure was maintained to urge public agencies to control and limit outdoor relief.[2] While this constant pressure resulted in some reform, public relief was still quite extensive two generations later.

The state guaranteed institutional care to people with settlements. In Boston they could be provided with food, fuel, and clothing through the Overseers of the Poor. In addition, the police stations provided free soup and temporary lodging for the needy. Thus, in 1870, a person with a settlement would be allowed limited outdoor relief in goods. Anyone, however, could get help from the police. Since the police kept no records, it was conceivable that a person, wanting nothing more, could go from station to station indefinitely.[3]

The settlement laws were relaxed in 1874 so that the residency requirement for public relief was five years rather than ten, the required years of tax payment were reduced from five to three, and women were granted rights apart from their husbands. These changes resulted in a doubling of settlement cases. As a means of judging the fitness of applicants, the Overseers established a wood yard and demanded two hours of labor by able-bodied men before they could receive dinner. This work test was believed to have reduced by ten thousand the number of meals served over the previous year. The public officials were so pleased with the results that by 1878 they considered light labor for women and other such tests as mandatory before free room and board would be given.[4]

Perhaps the most important contribution of a public agency in the final decades of the century was the gathering of statistics on the unemployed. While it may have been easy enough to tell that a depression was occurring once it was well advanced, it was extremely difficult to measure the depth of intensity of a crisis without reliable statistics. Until the late 1870s speculation was the only measure. In 1878 Carroll D. Wright, chief of the Massachusetts Bureau of Statistics of Labor, compiled the first systematic statistics on unemployment. Relief agencies by 1893 could be certain about the magnitude of the crisis.[5]

But aside from Carroll Wright's labor statistics, there were no innovations that might help with major depressions. The program of the Overseers of the Poor was designed only to handle ordinary community needs. Economic depression was to be met like any other special emergency—fire, flood, or natural disaster; an emergency committee would meet the need. Such committees, standing between the normal functions of public and private agencies, evince the groping of Bostonians toward the amelioration of industrial crisis.

Community relief efforts in 1873 clearly illustrate the general confusion about economic depression. Aid for victims of the economic disorder was confounded with aid to sufferers from the fire of a year earlier. The Summer Street fire, having destroyed many workrooms in the garment industry, made it difficult to distinguish unemployment and suffering from the fire from that caused by economic distress. Indeed, until 1874 few people took the depression seriously. Some thought the storm was over, just as it was beginning. "Everyone agrees," claimed one observer, "that the panic is over, and that matters will rapidly adjust themselves. I see no symptoms of distress or alarm in Boston. It has been but a squall, in comparison with the tornado of '57." But the fire meant much. With the fresh memory of the Chicago disaster, Bostonians turned to show that they, too, could sweep up the ashes.[6]

Awe of the fire and a sense of civic virtue brought Bostonians to the support of the Fire Committee that was immediately established. The community effort was invigorating to some, for it proved "that Boston . . . is still governed by an aristocracy. Some of 'The Best' called a public meeting, & forth came Mr. William Gray & others & directed the Mayor."[7] Annie Fields was impressed by the "most fearful fire New England has ever known." For days there seemed to be alarms in every quarter of the city, as Mrs. Fields and "The Best" concentrated their energies on relief of the suffering in the burnt district. They brought food to them; but more important, they were able to reestablish emergency workrooms two months after the fire. "Poor women rush in for work," Mrs. Fields at last reported, "and I am happy with the result."[8]

William Gray, according to James Freeman Clarke and Mrs. Fields, directed the mayor to establish an emergency fire-relief committee and to place Otis Norcross at its head. Norcross and the committee began with a limited sum of money for the specific relief of those distressed by the fire. Aside from small amounts directed to help in the reestablishment of workrooms, most was spent for clothes, food, shelter, and transportation to assist relocation. The committee used the facilities of the Provident Association, requisitioning clothing and other supplies from the Provident's stores and distributing them to the needy. Efforts were made to reimburse other private agencies for aid. By the spring of 1873, however, the committee considered its task accomplished. Otis Norcross communicated this to the Provident Association, giving the Association $2,000 for a special fund to aid any remaining victims.[9]

Several private societies expressed concern over the special demands put on them. Few, however, acknowledged, in these early years, the existence of an economic depression. By the early months of 1876, however, the Provident had become aware that the emergency had not ended with the fire. The economic crisis had expanded and deepened to the point where the Association was pressed to the limits of its resources. Robert C. Winthrop anxiously wrote to Otis Norcross. A meeting of the managers of the Association, Winthrop reported, "found that our expenditures for charity had been greater than ever before & were rapidly exceeding our means. The want of work & wages," Winthrop continued, "has rendered destitute great numbers who have never begged before." He begged for relief from the fire fund to help save the Provident.[10]

It was to end this embarrassment of the Provident that Mrs. Fields wrote a public appeal for funds. She thought it a civic duty to raise money to help pay the Provident's huge relief bill. Yet, she insisted that "twenty five or thirty thousand dollars may be better employed than in giving food and clothing to the healthy poor because they cannot get work." She asked for work tests and other guarantees that funds are properly spent. But, more particularly, she suggested the need for planned public works.

"Are our streets so well kept," she demanded, "that we never need more workmen—Are the roads of Massachusetts more perfect than the roads of any other country that we can afford to throw away $20,000 a year without return?" Boston had much to be done, she claimed—a new sewage system under the Common "to stay the hand of pestilential fever which threatens our city." She found no excuse for the community supporting men in idleness. Before another autumn "we should lay some plan either for employing our own strength or sending it westward to strengthen other states. This year we have succeeded only in impoverishing ourselves."[11] She insisted that there be better planning should such a crisis recur.

The relief societies of Boston had little precedent for the crisis of 1873. True, the Society for the Prevention of Pauperism had met the panic of 1857 and suffered through it. But the SPP had insisted that the fault was within the individual. The Provident Association had considered this earlier crisis as a temporary failure of distribution. Thus, they were unprepared for a depression which would last throughout most of the decade.[12]

Faced with the reality of the crisis, there were those who

would not believe in it. The Provident Association found it difficult, even after the depression was well advanced, to separate it from the effects of the Summer Street fire.[13] The increased activity, however, began to tell. By 1874 the Provident Association had to draw on its invested funds. By 1876 the Provident was in such dire financial straits that it called on the city for help. The Association began to think of reforming its method of operation.[14]

The Provident Association lost control under the pressure of increased demand and seemed unable to manage the distribution of relief. To recover, it first tried restriction. Early in 1876 the Association redistricted so that "no section should include more than twenty poor families more or less." Gradually, professional visitors were hired to replace volunteers. By 1877 its work had been concentrated in the central office at the Charities Building, so as to limit reliance on inexperienced volunteers. Relief rolls were further reduced by demanding applications only from the male head of the family, where one existed. The Provident rid itself of some cases by requesting Catholics to appeal to their clergy. But still the crowds were so large at Chardon Street that a policeman had to be put on duty there to keep order.[15]

Doubtless, these economies had to be made if the Association was to continue. Yet, stringency and higher administrative costs were bound to bring public criticism. The Provident Association in the next decade was often forced to defend its high cost of giving relief.[16] It asserted that it deserved applause for its new methods of control.[17]

But apparently most Bostonians shared Annie Adams Fields's belief that better planning was necessary. For when the new crisis occurred in 1893–94, they met it with a peculiar combination of private relief and public works. In mid-December 1893, noting high unemployment, the Mayor called a meeting of citizens who recommended the establishment of a special citizens' committee to handle the emergency.

The Citizens' Relief Committee was made up of fourteen public-spirited citizens, many of them officers of charitable societies, including the Associated Charities. "There was no representative of workingmen's organizations upon the committee." The Committee members served without pay and hired their staff from the ranks of the unemployed. A public appeal for $100,000 was oversubscribed. All told, the Committee had $136,568.70 at its disposal over that emergency winter.[18]

Since the Committee's first task was to find suitable employment for men and women, it canvassed city departments to determine what could be done in the winter. The street department agreed to supply tools and supervision if the Citizens' Committee would furnish gangs of men. The Board of Health listed eighty-six alleys and small private streets which were not cared for by the city but were in unsanitary condition; these were to be cleaned by teams of unemployed men. The sewer department had intended to construct seventeen sewers in the coming spring. But a plan was developed by which the city agreed to have reputable contractors supply tools and supervision at normal summer prices and to hire, so far as possible, emergency men chosen by the Committee. Because of the difficulty of the winter season a reasonable profit had to be guaranteed.

Indoor work for women and less robust men proved a greater problem, for their work, it was felt, should not interfere with established industries. Almost everything had some difficulty; either it competed with someone's labor, or it entailed sending unknown and sometimes questionable people into private homes and buildings. The solution was making rag carpets, crazy quilts, and, for inmates of a charitable asylum, some white sewing. The argument for making these carpets and quilts was that there "was no demand for them, and therefore there was no considerable industry of that kind to be disturbed." Paradoxically, the qualification that made rug manufacture feasible made economy unlikely. "Looked at in whatever light one will," the Board report concluded, "the indoor work was hardly less than charity, —but charity with a quasi work test attached. The members of the Citizens' Relief Committee came to recognize it as such." At least one advantage of the indoor work was that little or nothing had to be expended by the Committee for materials, since most of the rags and tools were obtained through public solicitation.[19]

Male applicants for relief work were to report to the Old Court House, the women to workrooms on Bedford Street. Those ineligible for relief, and those of questionable character, were rejected out of hand. Applicants were required to have lived more than sixty days in Boston, to have others dependent on their labor, and to be of good character. The applicant's word was taken in an interview; the interviewer, however, could reject without explanation. The Committee hoped to verify claims through domiciliary investigation and inquiry at former places of employment. Actually, the magnitude of the task made such an investigation impossible. On sum, there were 7,460 male applicants, 5,761 of whom were offered work; 3,479 of the 4,566 women who applied at the various workrooms were given employment.[20]

The men received a dollar a day for indoor and ordinary outdoor jobs; the more strenuous labor on the sewers earned one dollar fifty cents a day. The women received seventy-five or eighty cents a day, depending on their workroom and their skill. They were expected to work nine hours a day and were divided into three shifts so that employment could be spread around and people would not become satisfied with relief work. At such a rate $86,775 was paid—$52,153 to men and $34,622 to women.[21]

While these figures would suggest that the men averaged $9 for the whole winter season, they were deceptive because some men made considerably less, some much more. A cigar maker, for instance, earned $24, a fisherman $23.25, and two junk dealers averaged $21 each. "Yet it remains true," the *Report* admitted, "that in actual dollars and cents the relief was hardly more than insignificant." This conclusion was inevitable since the average man, according to testimony, had been out of work for three months without odd jobs and without savings, and was alone responsible for the support of four persons. "To such men, an income of $10 in fragments two to four weeks apart could not have seemed large enough to call for a demonstration of very keen appreciation."[22]

Indeed, few were pleased with the program. Many problems had not been anticipated. Outdoor projects were expensive during the winter and of questionable value when done with inexperienced and transient help. Freezing made surface excavation difficult. Building brick sewers required special care during cold months; "the mere presence of frost in certain materials makes construction so unsafe that artificial heating is necessary."[23] The indoor projects, designed to avoid competition, were of little value. The Committee expended $53,896 in indoor enterprises and received $3,276 for goods manufactured. The deficit reflected both the small value of the product and the fact that most of the goods were given to charitable institutions. The workrooms, especially, caused the Committee anxiety. They did not want to give "charity work," a mere test of intent. They had hoped that the product of the labor would have intrinsic value, but they could not imagine such production that would not be competitive. The Committee finally came to understand their indoor and outdoor efforts to be charity and nothing more. It was a reluctant recognition. "If the committee had seen any other way to avoid a deficit,—any way to turn this resource over and over again, employing and re-employing labor,—it would have adopted it."[24]

Little in the report of the Board suggested that the relief

work was a good thing. Construction done for the city bene-
fited the community and, therefore, was not a loss. The jobs
created by the Committee also employed teamsters, and
others, who were not applicants for relief and who might
otherwise have been unemployed. Yet there was no suggestion that a public-works program that operated at a loss
was anything but charity; deficit spending could not be
justified in the minds of these men and women. Rather, the
question that dominated the Board's investigation, reflecting
the temper of the participants, was, should this relief work,
which was charity, be handled by established private organizations in the future, or should special committees for helping unemployed be used in subsequent emergencies? The
testimony varied only slightly in response to this question.[25]
Few people liked the Committee, but it is difficult to tell
how much of their revulsion was toward the emergency itself
rather than to inefficiency.

Robert Treat Paine, president of the Associated Charities,
was one of the few whose published testimony questioned
the wisdom of allowing established agencies with additional
funds to handle such crises. The emergency, according to
Paine, required special programs. He insisted that "the problems of employing the unemployed, and of relieving distress
and treating pauperism, had better be . . . kept absolutely
distinct." The established agencies, he asserted, were designed
to handle want and suffering, and it "would have been very
unwise to have obliged the laboring men and women . . . to
submit to the ordeal of the usual charity application." The
condition of Boston in the winter months necessarily limited
the amount of employment that could be offered, yet it was
better to provide this little work than to refer ten thousand
persons to organizations that had nothing in the line of jobs
to offer.

Paine asserted that it was the responsibility of the city,
or society in its "unorganized capacity," to provide "against

suffering, and the best way is to provide employment." In his judgment, "in time of great distress, normal industry stops and normal employment of labor does not exist, it is impossible to find employment to give labor, unless some special provision is made." To give this task to private agencies, he insisted, "would be asking the charitable societies to do a work they are not adapted to do." Paine did not expect, however, that an emergency relief committee would be needed for the following winter, "because there can be no sudden emergency this year." This was not to say that the depression had passed. Rather, hardship had been anticipated. But the unemployed were spread, according to Paine, throughout the country and the West. "They are being scattered where they can take care of themselves, and we shall not have, therefore, that emergency that will call for a Relief Committee."[26]

Paine's point of view was singular in the Board's report. William P. Fowler, chairman of the Overseers of the Poor, believed that with additional funds the established agencies and the Overseers could have met the need better than the emergency committee. After all, it had been charity; why disguise it? He believed that the relief would have been less demoralizing had it been given without work. "I don't believe," he said, "there is much gain by sugar-coating a pill— that is, by clothing it under the guise of work." Fowler insisted that new agencies should not be established when the older ones, with additional funds, could serve the purpose. He especially objected to the gross handling of the problem as the Emergency Committee was forced to do. Miss Annette P. Rogers, of the Admission Committee at Bedford Street, agreed with Fowler on this point. "It should not be possible," she said, "to attempt to aid so mixed a multitude, which was the reason that those most skilled and most self-respecting would not come to it."[27]

The testimony of Zilpha Smith, general secretary of the Associated Charities, is notable not only because it differed sharply from that of the president of her organization, but also because it questioned the very need of the relief itself. Miss Smith recognized some need existed in December, "perhaps as much because of the agitation . . . as from real need, but I was disappointed in the results of the relief work." Her principal objection was that "the whole matter was public from the beginning," thus attracting great numbers who were chronically dependent.[28] Miss Smith would have preferred having tickets in the neighborhoods to be given by persons who knew the applicants, like ministers and dispensary physicians. "You would reach a larger portion that need to be helped; and, whether you reach them all or not, if you actually help those you touch, it would be better than to aid a great many inadequately. I would have the money raised privately, without newspaper advertising." Asked whether the machinery of the established agencies was adequate without an emergency committee, she responded: "If there had been no Relief Committee, there would not have been so many cases." She doubted if many deserving cases would have suffered "physically" had there been no committee. Suffering resulting from long periods of unemployment could not be handled by charities anyway. And she was convinced, finally, that the charitable organizations could have raised all of the necessary funds.[29]

The general feeling was for more routine and against the emergency-committee idea. As Zilpha Smith put it, "the private way, the quiet way."[30] The conclusion was easily reached by some that the crisis was largely artificial "and . . . much increased by factitious causes." Without newspaper advertising, for instance, much panic would have been avoided.[31] By the time of the recession of 1896, William Fowler recalled the Emergency Committee sadly and hoped it would not be repeated. The normal work could go on "without interference on the part of the sympathetic but inexperienced public."[32] The experiment, however, was not without a les-

son. The report of the investigating board observed: "This
problem must be looked upon as a more or less permanent
one. . . . Evidence is too clear that even in so-called normal
times there is an amount of non-employment which occasions
suffering."[33] In this final sentence of the *Report* dawns the
awareness of the industrial age; relief could no longer be
another kind of charity.

Dissatisfaction with the work of emergency committees
reflected a continuing distrust of relief handled by the whole
public. Essential to the charity reformer was the notion that
great care and control had to be exercised in helping the
poor. The depressions, however, challenged the charitable
societies to maintain their improved methods under the
stress of great numbers. Could private charities meet the demands of the industrial age? Consideration of the private
agencies' adaptations to these crises will illustrate the con-
ceptual limitations of the charity reform.

The result of their early experience in the 1870s was that
charitable organizations met the depression of 1893 with
calm, control, and efficient organization. They were quick
to notice the signs, although they blamed extraneous causes
such as growing population and immigration.[34]

Aside from its new methods, the Provident Association
thought increased numbers of new charities helped reduce
its case load; the hard times of the 1890s did not devastate the
Association as did the earlier panic. Mainly, control was
effected by the machinery of the Association and its readiness
to refuse applications.[35]

The Industrial Aid Society, the free employment agency,
was unexcited by the panic of 1893; it merely did what it
could. It recorded increased applications that year. In fact,
it noted that the increase was even larger than the statistics
indicated, since the agents had not been able "to take down
the names of all the applicants, owing to the press of business. They . . . simply put down the names of those whom it

seemed likely that we could help." While deplorable, the Society found the condition "by no means unprecedented." The answer was to increase its office staff and advertise more extensively for jobs. Indeed, if all of the private agencies increased activities and called on the public for donations, the crisis would surely be met. "Too much relief is quite as bad as too little." The Society could reduce its cases by not "assisting men who might be able to obtain work although at lower wages than they were formerly accustomed to."

It was easy for the IAS to find the basic problem. "Despite the numerous inventions and suggestions made by theorists or social economists, personal effort remains as the only real cure for the evils of non-employment . . . there is no royal way out. . . . There is no magician's wand of paternalism or socialism to wave over the whirlpool and still the troubled waters." At last, the Industrial Aid Society was quick to announce the end of the depression, and that "in most cases idle men are now idle from choice, not from necessity."[36]

The Society was satisfied with its work. And so was Professor Davis R. Dewey, of the Massachusetts Institute of Technology and commissioner of the state board to investigate the unemployment of 1894–95. Dewey asserted that a free employment agency was a good thing and that it should be free of city or state control. He believed that the Industrial Aid Society needed only to expand its intelligence resources and make better use of labor unions in the gathering of information.[37]

While most private relief agencies adjusted to industrial crisis by simple expansion of operations, there were some notable efforts to innovate. The Industrial Aid Society had anticipated, at least in discussion, the possibility of public works programs. It had considered trying, in the 1870s and 1880s, to organize city work so that its applicants might benefit. There was some success in the effort, but the Society ran into the problem of city patronage. Attempts were also made in these early years to organize labor gangs to keep the railroad right-of-ways clear of snow in the winter. This and other snow-clearing operations were standard emergency winter employment for the Society; but the IAS was opposed to any make-work programs.[38]

In 1895 the Industrial Aid Society tried the Detroit or Pingree plan of giving to the poor small lots on which to raise vegetables for their own use and sale. The Society had no thought of the plan's effect on the price of produce. Land was secured, a farmer hired to supervise, and fifty men and two women were given one-third-acre lots to cultivate. Every applicant had to bring credentials from some society to verify his worthiness and need. The experiment succeeded in giving the participants something to do and a "new zest in life." Each cultivator produced from forty to fifty bushels of vegetables, earning from fifty to eighty cents a bushel. Yet the plan was not tried another year. The cost of tillable land near enough to the city to be of use was expensive. Since the crop had to be rotated, the old land could not be used. So the experiment was dropped.[39]

A more significant innovation was the Provident woodyard, established in 1875. Mr. George James, of the Provident Association, started the woodyard to provide temporary work for the unemployed and a work test for the applicants of the Association. He operated the woodyard independently, employing about twenty-five men a day. The men were paid an especially low wage of ten cents an hour in order that the yard would not compete with industry or be a satisfactory alternative to regular employment. James operated the yard without a loss until 1879, when the Provident agreed to give him a small subsidy. The Provident was pleased with the work test; those who did not meet it were undeserving, making part of the charity judgment. The Provident refused to take over the yard when James gave it up in 1882, although it admitted the usefulness of the enterprise. It was sustained for a few years, however, by a private corporation.[40]

While the work-test concept appeared ideally suited to prove that many applicants were unworthy, the proof was quite deceptive. The Provident discovered that work tests raised new problems. The woman who knew she could sew and the man who knew he could cut wood might not look for regular employment, the Provident thought. "From which it follows that paupers may be made by giving charity work just as easily as by giving coal, clothing, cash, or anything else."[41] A special agent of the Industrial Aid Society accused the men working in the woodyard maintained by the Overseers of the Poor. While he found some willing to take jobs, many were hopeless, "as the men were wholly indifferent to their own welfare, caring only to obtain a shelter for the night and something to eat."[42]

If private relief agencies stood against make-work projects, they resisted even more labor's efforts to control itself. Few charity people were as convinced as the settlement workers that organized labor had brought about great progress for the working class. From the beginning, the Industrial Aid Society considered the real labor problem to be a lack of skilled American laborers, lack of cooperation between labor and management and the influx of foreign workers who deprived the native-born of their rightful earnings. Both capital and labor, according to the Society, seemed to misunderstand the situation, and labor aggravated things by organizing and threatening unrest. The best solution to industrial problems would be through cooperative capital and labor ventures which looked to profit sharing.[43]

The Society could recognize instances of wrongs done to labor. Yet there could be no reason for agitation in America, whatever the European condition. "If the laborer lacks the qualities that make the capitalist, it seems to be no reason why he should quarrel with his employers, or with his opportunities." Indeed, labor unrest was held to be essentially un-American. For, it was claimed, "when the workmen were all Americans . . . strikes and contests were unknown." The slight likelihood that foreign laborers would become capitalists made them discontent. If these foreigners "were all steady, sober, and skilled workmen, thrifty and economical, looking to the interest of their employers as well as their own, the strife would soon cease, and the community would be the gainers."[44]

Thus, the general anti-organized-labor attitude was disguised by a nativism which became more virulent. If wages were low or there was unemployment, it was because the labor market was crowded by Chinese and "paupers from Europe." The situation called for "such laws and regulations as will best promote the welfare of our own people." As time went on, it became increasingly important to shut off the flow of immigrants to this country. "When hordes of uncivilized Poles, Bohemians, or other nationalities, soured and discontented . . . come here with poison and dynamite, boycotts and menace, to disturb our peaceful industries," Americans would be unmanly, "if we submitted without resistance." And when, the IAS railed, foreigners seek to disaffect American workmen "with a condition which we know to be the most equal and wise . . . we should not deserve our blessings if we did not visit with the most condign punishment such outrages, or drive out like mad dogs those that perpetrate them."[45] In calmer tones, it was reasoned that there were natural laws of the market that regulated wages, as other economic phenomena. Thus, the immigrant and labor agitator hurt labor, because one drove the wages down while the other involved the worker in useless and destructive activity. The employer, after all, would pay only what he thought the workers' services to be worth; "any coercion or other interference would put an end to work, and drive capital to other countries."[46]

Such sentiments about foreigners contributed to the nativist

rhetoric which was common in popular statements about industrial disputes. In this way, charity reform organizations
served the growing pressure for immigration restriction. The
charity reformers, however, were ambivalent when it came to
the matter of closing the gates to foreign migration. The
Bostonians, in general, spoke for a class that was meeting
serious political challenge from its immigrant population,
and most would attribute social unrest to new people who
were unfamiliar with the American way. Yet they also accepted, with little question, the notion that cheaper cost to
business (i.e., cheap foreign labor) meant rapid industrial
expansion which, in turn, meant greater progress and more
jobs. The same laissez-faire and "wages-fund" economic doctrine used to argue against organized labor made it difficult
to support immigration restriction. Nevertheless, the National
Conference on Charities and Corrections occasionally had
appeals for legislation restricting immigration. Robert Treat
Paine, along with Charles Warren, Prescott F. Hall, and
Robert DeCourcy Ward, was an organizer of the Immigration
Restriction League in 1894. Although all of these men served
eleemosynary societies, only Paine and, perhaps, Joseph Lee
among the founders of the League might be considered a
part of the charity organization movement as well. In time,
social workers, influenced by the settlement workers, mod-
erated their attitude toward foreigners. By 1910, John Higham notes, "very few social workers who had intimate contact with foreign groups favored a further restriction of
immigration."[47]

This antilabor attitude pervaded the charity movement. It
was against this sentiment that Mrs. McCallum, of the London charity organization movement, spoke when she defended the "radicals" of her Society who "feel that the salvation, not only of the working class, but of right principles of
charity, lies in cooperation with the trade-unions."[48]

With the same intent, Anna Garlin Spencer, minister and

reformer, spoke to defend the charity organization movement and scientific charity against attacks by labor and settlement people. Miss Spencer noted the applause that a labor leader received when he described a charity conference as "a place where men in swallow-tail coats and women in velvet and diamonds, who spend $10,000 a year, meet to tell men and women who can't earn ten dollars a week how to spend their money." Miss Spencer countered by insisting that the real labor question "does not rise into view until the untrained, the incompetent, the dishonest and the lazy are separated from the trained, the thrifty, the honorable and the energetic in the count." Even so, her remarks still had that "chill" of the modern benevolence which moved John Boyle O'Reilly to write of

That Organized Charity, scrimped and iced,
   In the name of a cautious, statistical Christ.[49]

Perhaps the interests of charity made it critical of the aims and methods of organized labor. Doubtless, the Provident Association was correct when it observed: "Were it not for the strikes by the labor unions the charities would have been still less; for, while the unions are supposed to help their members during strikes, they do nothing for non-members who consequently are thrown into idleness."[50]

The Industrial Aid Society, more than any other relief agency, theorized about economics. It managed always to support a conservative position, conceiving of an always limited wealth with a determined wages fund. No amount of agitation could increase that fund—higher wages for some meant lower wages for others. Economics was a matter of natural law, and the dynamic of that law was competition. The only way that a man could really increase his income was to implement and improve his skills. Thus, training and self-improvement were the answer to economic as well as moral problems. Any reform which did not effect self-improvement would be disruptive.[51]

But the organization was not consistent. While it could rail against immigrant labor at one time, earlier its reports supported the importation of Negroes and Chinese for domestic work. It had argued that the cheaper labor would be good competition and force increased efficiency. Furthermore, the money saved in low wages could go into other business, creating new work. But in later years the Society urged shipping labor out of the state and moving families from Boston.[52]

The Industrial Aid Society, like the other relief agencies, drifted through three decades of crisis, fitting its assumptions and prejudices to changing conditions. It was not a successful means of discovering methods to handle the unfamiliar. Indeed, the result of experience seemed to be negative judgment; they refused to accept what would not fit.

Private relief agencies, therefore, rejected public works and emergency committee methods of handling depression, and they were equally unreceptive to any program that might have given workers, through organized labor, more control in the economy. Their solution, again in Zilpha Smith's words, was to seek the "private way, the quiet way." It will be well to ask how reasonable this solution was in light of the problem.

It is quite clear that the relief agencies did not consider themselves emergency organizations. It is true that they often spoke of the necessity for laboring men to save and prepare for hard times, yet these organizations conceived of no special machinery for times of crisis. They only enlarged their existing programs as fast as possible, while maintaining reasonable discrimination. They tried to do what they normally did, but more.

By the very nature of depression the relief agencies' normal operation became more difficult. The Industrial Aid Society could not find jobs for men in the very industry that had made them unemployed. Despite the testimony of Zilpha Smith, it was hard to raise money during and after depressions; low interest rates reduced the resources of alms-giving agencies.[53] Indeed, the very need compromised the private agencies' ability to serve.

Significantly, the history of these relief agencies seemed to work against aiding the laboring man who was thrown out of work by a depression. They actually preferred to work with the marginal man who might be unemployed if not given the extra push, who did not know his strengths and what facilities were open to him, who might fall into pauperism without a necessary goad and, of course, the man who was the imposter and had to be exposed. The emphasis had always been reform and uplift. As one Society put it, "We deal with the incapables. . . . Our agents go out and make personal intercession with employers of labor, urging the crying need of the applicant, and appealing to every possible motive which can influence a favorable reply." Such organizations would not attend to programs to alleviate suffering in a depression. And working men would hardly find real relief in their offices.[54]

NOTES

1. Leah Hannah Feder, *Unemployment Relief in Periods of Depression* (New York, 1936), passim, discusses national reaction to these depressions.
2. Ibid., Ch. 3. The greatest pressure was exerted by the Associated Charities after 1879.
3. Ibid., Ch. 3,
4. Boston Overseers of the Poor, *Annual Report*, XI (May 1875), 6; XII (May 1877), 7, 13; XIV (May 1878), 11.
5. Massachusetts Bureau of Statistics of Labor, *Report*, X (January 1879), 3–13; Feder, *Unemployment Relief*, 38–39; James Leiby, *Carroll Wright and Labor Reform* (Cambridge, Mass., 1960), esp. Ch. 3.
6. Letter from Francis E. Parker to Samuel Gray Ward, November 14, 1873, Parker papers, Houghton (fire compared with Chicago's in letter

from James Freeman Clarke to Sarah F. Clarke, November 18, 1872, Clarke papers, Houghton).

7. Letter from Clarke (see preceding note); Fields also mentions Gray's control of the Mayor (Diary, November 21, 1872).

8. Fields, Diary, November 10 and 21, 1872; December 1, 1872; and February 1, 1873.

9. Letter from Otis Norcross to Robert C. Winthrop, April 4, 1873, Norcross papers, MHS (this letter is quoted in Provident, *Report*, XXII [1873], 6–7); Provident, "Records," April 11 and December 5, 1873, and March 6, 1874, indicate that the money went into a special fire fund, although the published *Report* contradicts. The Provident also received the residue of the fire fund in 1858 ("Records," March 4, 1858).

10. The fire discomfited CFS (*Report*, XXXIX [1873], 1–2), F&WS (*Report*, LVI [1873], 5), and IAS (*Report*, XXXVIII [1873], 5–6). Letter from Robert C. Winthrop to Otis Norcross, February 15, 1876, Winthrop papers, MHS.

11. Annie Adams Fields, draft of a letter, no addressee, n.d., Fields's papers, MHS.

12. SPP, *Report*, XXII (1857), 15–17; Provident "Records," January 7 and November 4, 1858.

13. Letters from Francis E. Parker to Samuel Gray Ward, November 14 and December 31, 1873, Parker papers, Houghton; the latter letter claimed that the panic was "quite over." Provident, *Report*, XXV (1876), 7–8.

14. Provident, "Records," March 6, 1874; March 10, April 7, and May 5, 1876; *Report*, XXIV (1875), 1–2.

15. Provident, "Records," April 7 and May 5, 1876, and February 16 and April 13, 1877; *Report*, XLIX (1900), 7–8, for a statement on how rolls were reduced.

16. "An Expensive Charity," Boston *Herald*, November 11, 1885 (also extract of letter from S. B. Cruft to the Provident, December 11, and reply December 14, 1886, among the papers of the Boston Family Service Association); Provident, *Report*, XXXVI (1887), 9–10.

17. Provident, *Report*, XXXI (1882), 7–10.

18. Massachusetts Board to Investigate the Subject of the Unemployed, *Report* (Boston, 1895), House Document No. 50, pt. 1, "Relief Measures," 12–13, hereinafter cited as Massachusetts Unemployed, *Report*.

19. Ibid., 22–24; quoted, 23–24.

20. Ibid., 21; see testimony of Francis C. Lowell, p. 35, for problems of registration and investigation. All figures for women and total male applicants only (see p. 17, tables); for number of men offered work see p. 26. Question remains as to the significance of these figures: how many men offered work took it?

21. Ibid., 26 (figures).

22. Ibid., 26–28. Some women tended to lower general wages because relief work permitted them to underbid others in ordinary employment (see testimony of Miss A. P. Rogers of the Admissions Committee, p. 30).

23. Ibid., xxviii.

24. Ibid., 25.

25. Ibid., 27.

26. Ibid., 33–35 testimony of Robert Treat Paine.

27. Ibid., 37–38, testimony of William P. Fowler; 38, of Annette P. Rogers.

28. This assertion is not substantiated by the *Report:* 74.95% of the applicants had not been aided by any of the private agencies which reported to the Associated Charities; they were new cases.

29. Massachusetts Unemployed, *Report*, 38–39, testimony of Zilpha D. Smith.

30. Ibid., 39.

31. Overseers of the Poor, *Report*, XXXI (February 1, 1894, to January 1, 1895), 10.

32. Ibid., XXXIII (February 1, 1896, to January 1, 1897), 13.

33. Massachusetts Unemployed, *Report*, pt. 4, "Causes," pp. iii–iv.

34. Edward Everett Hale blamed early signs of distress on the large immigration of poor Russians (IAS, "Records," January 20, 1892); a year later it was observed that unemployment resulted from influx of Portuguese, Italians, Canadians, and Irish (Provident, *Report*, XLII [1893], 11–12).

35. Provident, *Report*, XLII (1893), 9–10; "Records," February 13, 1894; Associated Charities, "Records," February 9, 1894.

36. IAS, "Records," January 17, 1894; *Report*, LVIII (1893), 6–7; LIX (1894), 5–6; LX (1895), 5–6.

37. IAS, "Report of Special Managers' Meeting," March 8, 1897.

38. IAS, "Executive Committee Reports," December 22, 1876, August 2, 1877, March 13, 1882, February 4, 1884; *Report*, XLI (1876) and XLII (1877), for general discussion of work relief (but see Overseers of the Poor, *Report*, XIV [May 1878], 48, for special snow-clearance project); XLVIII 1883), 9–10, for attitudes on made work.

39. IAS, "Special Meeting of the Executive Committee," April 10, 1895; *Report*, LX (1895), 6–7; LXI (1896), 6; another farming plan discussed by this Society, "Records," April 20, 1898.

40. Provident, "Records," December 10, 1875, January 7, 1876, February 14, 1879, February 11, 1881, March 9 and 23, and November 10, 1882; *Report*, XXXI (1882), 9&n: the Overseers' woodyard did not pay money, but rather was a test for board and lodging; XXXIII (1884), 6–7, a general assessment.

41. Provident, *Report*, XXIX (1880), 9–10.

42. IAS, *Report*, LXIV (1899), 8.

43. Woods, *City*, 282; SPP, *Report*, XXXII (1867), 8–10; XXXIII (1868), 8; XXXIV (1869), 10–12. The IAS's reports contained long statements on industrial problems and economic theory.

44. IAS, *Report*, XXXV (1870), 11, 14. (See also Otis Norcross, "Diary," July 27, 1877, Norcross papers MHS, for similar views regarding the B & O, Pennsylvania, and Reading railroad riots.)

45. Ibid., XLIX (1884), 7–8; LI (1886), 15.

46. Ibid., LII (1887), 7.

47. John Higham, *Strangers in the Land* (New Brunswick, 1955), 120.

48. Mrs. McCallum, "Address to the Annual Meeting of the Associated Charities," November 1893, from typescript among "Records" of that organization.

49. Quoted by Mrs. Anna G. Spencer, "Address to the Annual Meeting of the Associated Charities," from a typescript dated November 10, 1898, appended to the "Records" of that organization.

50. Provident, *Report,* LI (1902), 8.

51. IAS, *Report,* LI (1886), 13–15; LII (1887), 9–10.

52. SPP, *Report,* XXXI (1866), 14–15; XXXIII (1868), 16; XXXIV (1869), 13–15; IAS, *Report,* XXXV (1870), 15–16; XXXIX (1874), 4–5; LXII (1897), 5–6.

53. Evidence for the difficulty of fund raising can be found in Miss Smith's own Associated Charities; it almost expired in the late 1890s. See Associated Charities, "Records," September 14 and December 14, 1894; July 8 and August 12, 1898; "Administrative Committee Report," October 12 and November 30, 1898; see also Otis Norcross, "Diary," October 18, 1875, for a different instance.

54. Quoted from IAS, *Report,* LIX (1894), 7–8; this point of view was common: IAS, "Executive Committee Report," November 6, 1893, January 1, 1894, March 4, April 1, and May 6, 1901; Provident, *Report,* XLI (1892), 9, and XLIV (1895), 9.

7

Two Cities and Charity:
The Infirm Bridge

WILLIAM ELLERY CHANNING considered the city a commonwealth in which all men served the ideal community. The
fractioning effect of economic and social class was to be contained by the ligaments of Christian charity. Bound together
by moral obligation, givers and receivers alike were to serve
the community. At the end of the nineteenth century, much
of the tautness had disappeared from Channing's liberal
Christianity. Boston, expanded by immigration and changed
by industry, had fragmented the community and lacked a single ideal to which everyone could respond.

Those whose roots were in Boston's past found that their
language and values were not universally understood; their
ideals seemed to stand for little against the realities of poverty. This alienation provoked anxieties reflected in philanthropic activities. The charity organization movement reiterated traditional standards. The individuals active in reform
brought to their work assumptions that they translated into
demands for social behavior.

Two people are ideal for illustration: Annie Adams Fields,

one of Boston's leading reformers, and Charles Russell Codman, after 1879 the president of the Provident Association. Both gave much of their lives to social service, both were reared in the shadow of Channing's influence, and both had family connections stemming from the first establishments in Massachusetts. Annie Adams's family went back to Henry Adams of Braintree, who came to Massachusetts in 1633. Codman had a paternal ancestor on the *Mayflower* and was connected maternally to the New York Knickerbockers. The ideals and values that shaped their lives derived from a native tradition.[1]

Essential to many reformers was the ideal of self-perfection through work and study. Man was perfectible, and it was his duty to improve himself and help in the uplift of others. Mrs. Fields's life exemplified this demand. Her marriage and life with James T. Fields, the publisher, was devoted to the cultivation of their literary interests and talents. Her Charles Street home was a salon for notable literary figures. And her diary, which she kept from 1863 to 1876, was a record of the vagrant thoughts of great men and women: Emerson, Whittier, Lowell, George William Curtis, Harriet Beecher Stowe, Oliver Wendell Holmes, Louis and Alexander Agassiz, Lydia Maria Child, Henry James, Thackeray, Dickens, Landor, Clemens, Bret Harte. After James T. Fields retired in 1870, Mrs. Fields helped develop a series of orations which made him one of the most popular circuit lecturers of the time. She often accompanied him on his tours. Childless, she was left alone when Fields died in 1881, but she continued her literary activity. Indeed, she began to publish her poetry and biographical sketches of her friends. In her late years she was the companion of Sarah Orne Jewett.

Perfection of self meant more to Mrs. Fields than the expression of intellectual interests or talents. Her idea is clear in her interpretation of Théophile Gautier's insistence that man learn to "play his intellectual instrument and to bring it to the farthest point of perfection!!!" Annie Fields was compelled to "put this sentence 'into our life' as the Dutch-man sayeth." This truth went beyond the sense of the poet. It could not, for her, mean only the "intense intellectual drudgery and selfish absorption of the litterateur." There was meaning here also for the "philanthropist or even a woman!!! a housekeeper, the mother of children." She found the finest expression of this "truth" in the life of a woman missionary whom she knew. A kind of martyr, this woman's self-sacrifice was especially beautiful to Mrs. Fields. For it was a distinct case of the "intellectual instrument be-ing brought to its finest perfection by continued use and without conscious effort to *this* end." Here was a strictly moral effort, "the instrument being regarded simply as such, and not as the poor little litterateur considers, a superior and peculiar gift to be petted for its own sake."[2]

Or, a passage from *Wilhelm Meister* pleased her, where Goethe had revered the " 'individual who understands dis-tinctly what he wishes, who unwearily advances, who knows the means conducive to his object, and can seize and use them.' " As Mrs. Fields saw it, the problem was a balance between thought and action, art and production; the in-dividual had to decide which to emphasize.

Mrs. Fields considered it her first duty "to serve others unselfishly according to the example of our dear Lord." Her second object was self-realization: "to cultivate my powers in order to achieve the highest life possible to me as an in-dividual existence by stimulating thought to its finest issues through reflection, observation and by profound and cease-less study." The simple, everyday questions had to be squared with these ends with "all the earnestness put into it of a creature who knows that the next moment he may be called to his account." As a woman and a wife, Mrs. Fields was obliged to her home: "to make that beautiful; to stimulate the lives of others by exchange of ideas, and the repose of

domestic life; to educate children and servants." Outside her
home, her duty was to the poor. "To be conversant with the
very poor; to visit their homes; to be keenly alive to their
suffering; never allowing the thought of their necessities to
sleep in our hearts." And, finally, "By day and night, morning and evening, in all times and seasons when strength is
left to us to study, study, study—." Study came last because
she saw the need of balance and social involvement; she did
not want to return to the ideals of the ancients, "so fine in
their results to the few, so costly to the many." Study and
knowledge were important to her, nevertheless. For, "in the
removed periods of existence when solitude may be our
blessed portion what a joy to fly to communion with the
sages and live and love with them." Thus she saw a life of
ideals, or morals and culture. "It is a wide plan, too wide
I fear for much performance but therefore perhaps more
conducive to a constant faith."

Although Mrs. Fields chose to mention only Europeans,
her commitment to self-perfection was very American. Gautier and Goethe may have been the immediate inspirations,
but the Puritan's obligation was the root. And she only had
to look in her own neighborhood to talk with Emerson
about self-reliance and the representative person. She shared
with her contemporary, Jane Addams, a very deep sense of
personal obligation to the community. They were both traditional enough, but Mrs. Fields was the more genteel.

The Puritan's conscience and the Transcendentalist's idealism were fused in Mrs. Fields. Her drive to self-perfection
was translated into community work. Prizing books, service
in good works, and obligation to family and home, the good
life was all delicacy and balance. She found no difficulty in
working for women's education and arguing for a domestic
training and career for women. Thus, when she met with
Mrs. Stowe and Miss Beecher to discuss a program for wom-
en's higher education they found it necessary to insist that

such a college teach domestic skills.[3] Women must train themselves, but they should remember that compared to the knowledge of men the knowledge of women was useless, since it had no special function.[4]

Most charity reformers responded to the same ideals as Mrs. Fields. But the obligation of self-perfection in a life less full than Mrs. Fields's could assume the intensity of compulsion. For example, Lillian Clarke, daughter of James Freeman Clarke, was thirty-eight and unmarried when she began to keep her diary. Her life was busy enough. She worked in the Infant Asylum, the New England Hospital, the Boston Dispensary, the Society for the Suppression of Vice and, like her father, with the women's-education part of the women's-rights movement. Perhaps it is too much to call her notebooks diaries. They were seldom more than a daily record of activities. A cramped and frugal hand told of trips to Boston, unsuccessful painting, meeting friends, work with societies; but it was merely a reporting hand which said little about what was felt or understood. The entries are terse and compulsive, seldom making judgments except to place quotes around Mrs. when an unwed mother is mentioned.

Lillian Clarke's efforts to bring her "instrument to perfection" was expressed in resolutions: on Sunday, January 28, 1883, she promised to her diary that she would not read novels, nor would she drink tea. She would sweep her room every morning and go to bed at nine o'clock. The following week she added coffee to her prohibitions, and further resolved, "If cross read no books for 24 hours." By the next week her errant spirit had apparently found escape from its literary confinement, for now she proscribed "parts of novels in magazines." After mentioning all of her earlier resolutions she concluded, "If I am able to keep these perfectly add another next week."[5]

Charles Russell Codman's young manhood, on the other hand, did not promise much effort toward self-perfection. In

Harvard's class of 1849, Codman was continually admonished
for "excessive unexcused absences from recitations" and "in-
decorum at chapel." In his sophomore year he was suspended
along with other boys for setting a bonfire before University
Hall. He was examined and readmitted after a winter's absence and allowed to graduate with his class. He excelled
in no way; his sole activity was the Harvard Whist Club,
which he enjoyed for its conviviality. He candidly remarked
of his college work: "I have not been distinguished as a
scholar, which . . . circumstance is attributable to an indolent temperament which can be overcome only by strong
exertion."[6]

What Codman's youth lacked in seriousness and exertion
he made up for as an adult in public service. In 1862 he
helped to organize the 45th Massachusetts Regiment. As
Colonel, he led it in campaigns in North Carolina. He did
not reenlist when the regiment was mustered out in 1863,
but rather entered state Republican politics. He served in
the state senate in 1864 and 1865. Later, he represented
Negro and wealthy constituents from Ward 6 (Beacon Hill
and part of Back Bay) in the state senate from 1872 to 1875.
He lost a very close mayoralty race to the Democrat Frederic
O. Prince in 1878. Liberal in his politics, Codman supported
tariff and civil-service reform and joined the mugwump bolt
to Grover Cleveland in 1884. A deeply religious man, Codman served Trinity Church as vestryman from 1869 to 1915
and for forty-two of those years acted as church warden.
Beside this and his work with the Provident, he was a trustee
of the Weston Insane Hospital, member and president of the
Harvard College Board of Overseers, and member of the
Massachusetts Historical Society and the State Board of In-
sanity. He balanced varied community service with his occupation in trusts and investment banking.[7]

This ideal of social obligation inspired many others in
charity reform. It was duty and a desire for selfless service,

for example, that spurred Mrs. Fields. It had compelled her to rally support for the Provident Society in 1875 when demands for relief had nearly sapped its resources. And her appeal was couched in the language of a "debt of honor" that the community must pay. Selflessness in public service inspired her to attack the Benthamite rejection of sentiments of unselfish benevolence and love of justice, replaced by an "educated intellect enlightening the selfish feelings." This utilitarian heresy she considered "the crying evil of our day."[8]

Sometimes, however, duty and obligation could become confused with business responsibility and achievement, especially when such service involved the investment of other people's money. Good business could become a public service. Thus, Francis E. Parker, trustee of the Industrial Aid Society, would sacrifice a customary holiday in Europe because "I made a promise that I could finish certain work before taking another vacation; and as far as not taking the vacation goes, I have left my word." He was obliged to a client. Parker felt amply rewarded, however, by the success of the business transaction, the reason for his sacrifice. There had been a flurry of land buying near Boston, and Parker wrote a friend, "I hardly liked being absent, while there was a chance to sell land (which I hold as Trustee)—to the great advantage of my friends." As it turned out, Parker sold twelve acres for $61,500 from a thirty-two acre parcel, all of which had been assessed at $9,000 seven years earlier. He estimated that the remaining twenty acres were worth at least $100,000. "So," he said, "I am very happy to have staid at home." Prosperity, good business, and social obligation were intimately associated in Parker's mind. He saw the rightness of a return to prosperity, "at least for those who were rich before," because the city has been "redeemed from [its] selfishness . . . by several noble gifts of money."[9]

Parker mixed good works with good business, as he was convinced it should be. He might mildly complain when he had to labor for a trustee, but in a few weeks he could report himself "enjoying my work, and as happy as is for our good in this world." Was this sense of obligation rare? Parker thought so. Compared with New Yorkers, Bostonians did well. The relative irresponsibility of New York wealth made Parker uncomfortable; he would not tarry in the society of the "New York swells."[10]

Beneath this drive for perfection and commitment to social service was a liberal Christian faith that lacked theological rigor. Mrs. Fields, for instance, professed some vague religion of humanity, a kind of Emersonianism, that could permit spiritualism, mysticism, and science to be fused together. When she spoke with Whittier about life and death she insisted on a "kernel of truth hidden in so-called spiritualism," which "came nearer to proving the outlet and inlet of Science than any other facts opening before us." The sciences, she felt, "seem to tend to materialism strictly." Spiritualism alone "deals with the mysterious between the seen and the unseen." The most notable statement recalled from a discussion about Herbert Spencer was an irrelevancy by Reverend Cyrus Bartol about the Trinity, that he could believe in it, *"if they could only make the Son large enough to signify all the children of men."* Mrs. Fields found this to be a beautiful idea, "not that *I* could ever give up, the representative man Christ, since the Lord has given us such a glorious example—but the other view has a fine truth sustained in it." And Mrs. Fields found a lecture by Louis Agassiz on embryology, its system and history, to form "an insuperable barrier in my own mind to the faith of Darwin."[11]

Charles Codman, on the other hand, placed his faith in progress, joining God's will to secular development. His faith allayed anxiety over industrial crisis. On reading Augustus Mongredien's pamphlet on economic change, Codman expressed faith in progress despite its attendant poverty. It was true, he claimed, that each new invention or discovery dislocated capital and labor. But no doubt "in time society adapts itself in the new condition of things, and even the laborers thrown out of work are only so thrown out temporarily; and society goes on all the richer and the more comfortable for the new invention." He thought it a law that some degree of poverty must accompany progress. "So as we can see," he said, " 'progress and poverty' must necessarily accompany each other for a time"; but progress being the larger stream would finally absorb the poverty that it creates. "Now there must always be progress in human affairs—we can set no limit on it—and it would seem . . . that poverty can never quite be extinguished."[12]

Thus Codman's faith in progress became a tenet of his Christian belief. For Jesus had said the poor would remain. Indeed, the very existence of poverty in time of prosperity made this Christian observation have "strange and wonderful" significance for Codman. For, when man gains in physical comforts, achieves moral heights, "nay even makes progress in spiritual life," along with this progress "distress comes which it is the Christian's duty and privilege to alleviate." Man could not, he insisted, be free of this obligation until the establishment of the promised kingdom of God on earth. Until then there would always be suffering to relieve.[13]

Thus poverty and charity were parts of a larger religious scheme. As Francis Parker saw benevolence as redemptive of civic avarice, Codman thought that charity could redeem the giver. Reading a novel by Howard O. Sturgis telling of a woman who had lived in sin, Codman wrote to the author that the woman's salvation was "to repent and to bring forth works. . . . I should say a single life devoted to good works was the only career open to her from which she could gain any satisfaction."[14]

The tendency to bind together religion, poverty, self-perfection, and civic duty often resulted in the romanticizing of the philanthropist and the poor. To Annie Adams Fields,

Mrs. Caswell, the missionary whose self-sacrifice she admired, was a perfect philanthropist. Mrs. Caswell was "almost destitute of what we know as culture." She has been brought up in the country by a "Calvinist or Methodist" father. And she had gone west to become a missionary among the Indians. There "by her sweet voice, her singing, by her loving and continued and persistent effort she drew the masses of the Indians around her and subdued them as no one else has ever been able to do," Mrs. Fields gushed.

After seventeen years Mrs. Caswell married and returned to Boston. Mrs. Fields met her and was impressed, not only with her story, but with her work among the poor of Boston. "Her power grows daily," Mrs. Fields claimed, "—she cultivates continually this influence she never thinks about except as she sees her continued efforts are crowned with continued success—and so she works on and on every day and every hour until the people lean upon her and flock about with their love."[15] Thus, rightly, in Mrs. Fields's view, this selfless service was rewarded by the gratitude of the poor. When Mrs. Caswell fell ill, Mrs. Fields went to visit her. It was a sad trip, to see a saint in her last moments. Her long years and days of work with the poor had brought her to her end. "Another martyr!" Mrs. Fields exclaimed. "How can we spare her sweet cheerful face?"[16]

Beauty was in such a sacrifice, as in poverty, borne well. Such, Mrs. Fields saw in Sainte-Beuve's biographical sketch of Mme. Desbordes-Valmore. She was moved to quote the lady:

> Let us not be overcome, however. It is easier to resign oneself to poverty when one feels with passion the sight of the sun, of the trees, of the gentle light, and holds the profound belief of seeing once again the dear ones whom one mourns.

"Is not this the ideal character!" Mrs. Fields exclaimed, "could there be anything more exquisite in this dark world?"[17]

Mrs. Fields's romantic view of poverty marked all of her work with the poor previous to that with the Cooperative Society of Visitors and the Associated Charities. She would devise schemes for the elimination of some evil and throw herself into its promotion, at least until it bored her. So it was with the Cooperative Building Committee's work against tenement evils, which she promoted in 1871. Her singular scheme, however, was the establishment of coffeehouses throughout the working-class sections of Boston. Open late at night, they served coffee for five cents a cup. The idea was to counteract whiskey drinking or, short of that, to give intoxicated men a place to regain their bearings. For two years her diary was filled with the work for these houses—collecting funds, assigning managers, and enlisting other sponsors. A limited success, with only one reported failure, she was anxious to be rid of them after two years. "I will be glad to get the Coffee Rooms finally launched [on their own], because the responsibility weighs. . . . Indeed, should one prove unsuccessful on my hands I should suffer."[18] She also supported the Working Women's Home on Lincoln Street. She worked hard for the Home, especially after the fire in 1872 when she used her influence with Otis Norcross to get it $200 for relief.[19]

These values would have been familiar enough to William Ellery Channing; the need for the perfecting of self, the obligation to community service, and the idealization of the charitable effort had motivated Channing too. But by the end of the century these ideals had become the special possession of a class. The city had fragmented—much as Channing had feared—so that those who worked with the poor found themselves estranged. Not only the immigrants, but native Bostonians had begun to feel strange in their city.[20]

Despite her duty and devotion to the poor, whenever Mrs. Fields reported coming in actual contact with them there was alienation, a chasm her sympathy could not bridge. This estrangement speaks through her reports of visits to the North End Mission, "where we did our best to amuse the poor."[21] It is suggested by her apprehension about controlling her charges of poor children on an excursion into the country; " 'If you speak to them in a low tone it will be all right.' " she was assured.[22]

She was easily moved by suffering. At Mrs. Augustus Hemenway's home she met a southern clergyman. "The war has [put] deep lines of suffering upon his face—he needs help for his school—I wonder where we shall find it for him."[23] But the same pity could betray Annie Fields when she hired a servant girl. "I have one of those sickly dull unfortunates who are a pain to see about, but she is so unfortunate that I took her from a sense that I was trying to do a good thing."[24]

Annie Fields expected sympathy to be repaid with gratitude; the recipient was as much obliged as the giver. Indeed, she considered benevolence, in itself, a force for the good— once done, it returned in many blessings. A desperate woman who threatened suicide would not, Mrs. Fields thought, because "The memory of what Bessie Greene has been to her is too strong."[25] Ingratitude, on the other hand, was keenly felt by her. When some working girls failed to attend a May Day party at the Lincoln Street home, she could not disguise her disappointment.[26] Toward the end of the 1870s, Mrs. Fields began to notice impositions by the poor.[27] They did not respond as she anticipated; they seemed a strange people who did not understand, and who would exploit.

Mrs. Fields was imposed upon, and it affected her deeply. After the fire of 1872 she helped Mrs. Margaret Murphy start a business. Mrs. Murphy's plan was to hire girls unemployed by the fire. Mrs. Fields left the management of the business in Mrs. Murphy's hands, but expected her to repay a $200 debt of honor. In 1874, however, the business failed. Mrs. Murphy, heavily in debt and pressured by her husband

("a hard man"), considered Mrs. Fields a partner and tried
to force her to assume the indebtedness. Mrs. Fields felt
threatened and was afraid. The matter was simple: "an Irish
woman in Boston . . . was endeavoring to extort money from
us." Mrs. Fields felt no obligation; she had done her best.
"Of course I did not persuade her, of course she can find no
case except that she owes me, or us, money which she never
means to pay, but the letter is full of hatred . . . and threat
that I cannot get it out of my mind. How strange it is that
our best efforts may end in this! God help us all." How could
charity conceive hatred?[28]

Mrs. Murphy finally forced the issue by coming to the
house. Since Mrs. Fields refused to talk to her, she waited
on the steps until Mr. Fields returned. "Imagine my agony.
I went up to my room . . . I feared a violent scene. I could
not tell what the end might be." Mr. Fields finally came,
talked coolly to the woman, demanded an apology for her
threatening letters, loaned her two hundred dollars and sent
her "rejoicing on her way." The matter was honorably resolved; Annie Fields was relieved. But she did not miss a lesson in the experience. "I had been too daring and head-
strong in aiding and abetting her desire to undertake the
business," she concluded. "Mr. Beal told me, *he had never
known a single instance* of money loaned in this way to do
any good." But it was over. She "lay down that night and
have ever since done so with lighter spirit."[29]

Annie Fields had learned that thoughtless aid was repaid
only by ingratitude and imposition. She discovered that selflessness could be harmful; one had to be discriminating in
the giving of self as well as goods. Thus, she was ripe for the
instruction of Octavia Hill and the charity organization
philosophy. Indeed, Mrs. Fields was well advanced in the
study of this reform when the crisis of 1873 seemed to call
for her and this special solution.

She responded with all of herself, becoming a stalwart of

the Associated Charities and one of America's leading advocates of charity organization principles. Mrs. Fields never
lost her sense of duty and service. But in these later years her
energy turned to work in organizations rather than for people. She still responded with sympathy to sights of poverty.
She could be overwhelmed by the helpless poor in England.[30]
And her interest could be attracted by special work with the
poor. She found Toynbee Hall to be a "noble foundation."
She doubted, however, whether the same thing could be tried
in America, the needs being different. "Though New York
probably comes nearer to it than we do in Boston where
we have a great deal of poverty, but we have no class to
whom our museums are inaccessible, the city is so much
smaller, and the impoverished better class cannot be said
to exist."[31]

Mrs. Fields's last will testified to her changed views toward
charity. Outside her immediate family and friends, Mrs.
Fields remembered only one individual, and that was an
afterthought. She pleaded with her beneficiaries to give Miss
Margaret Bolger, a dressmaker, five hundred dollars. Miss
Bolger was a good woman "now grown old and nothing
saved because she has supported a large family of penniless
nieces and nephews."[32] The rest of her estate was left to
organizations or institutions. She left $5,000 to Dartmouth
College, $6,000 to Portsmouth, New Hampshire, for the ben-
efit of the boys' and girls' public high schools, "each sum to
constitute a fund, the income of which shall be used for
scholarships for the purpose of advancing the higher education of really promising pupils who could not otherwise
afford to continue their studies," $5,000 to the Gwynne Tem-
porary Home for Children and $2,000 to the Old Peoples'
Memorial Fund, "established to assist aged and worthy persons." The largest money bequest, $40,000 was of course left
to the Associated Charities. Even here, the money was not to
aid the poor directly. Rather, it was to be invested and the

income distributed by the corporation, "as annual pensions
for . . . registrars and ward agents . . . who . . . shall . . . be
incapacitated by age, sickness or other infirmity." Mrs. Fields
specified that "Zilpha D. Smith and her sister, Frances A.
Smith . . . shall receive a pension amounting to at least one
third of the annual income of such fund."[33] Thus Mrs.
Fields's last efforts were to sustain the work of organizations
and charity workers. How distant from the poor's needs
"never to sleep in our hearts."

What happened to Mrs. Fields was experienced by others
also. The simple ideals of old were inadequate to the complexities of large-scale urban poverty. Whether they saw the
community as it divided between rich and poor, immigrant
and native, or Protestant, Catholic, and Jew, sympathy was
hard to communicate to all; the results of private benevolence were seldom gratifying. Channing's charity was an infirm bridge between classes. There were enough people of
wealth and good intention in Boston. There never seemed
to be a shortage of those who wanted to do good. But it took
more than a trip across town and the helping hand to touch
the poor. Changes in the society made the human distance
greater between the rich and poor than the geographic distance between their homes. Poor people were not merely
rich people with less money, ability, and opportunity. In
many ways they were in different societies altogether.

Settlement workers got some hint of this separation of cultures when they looked at the workings of ward politics.
They noticed, with amazing perception, that the ward boss
was something more than a corrupt political organizer to his
constituents. The boss would see that a family's rent was
paid, get legal assistance for an oppressed immigrant, arbitrate in local disputes, gain admission for the sick into hospitals, and guide friends around obstacles for admission into
trades schools. Distinguishing between the deserving and the
unworthy poor was simple for the boss; he helped those who

could help him. He would help a friend obtain church or municipal charity, regardless of the subtleties of the need. From the beneficiaries' point of view, he was a more enlightened philanthropist than those who worked in organizations and gave systematically their time, money, and advice.[34]

The boss had jobs to hand out as patronage. Even if he did not have long-term positions to offer, he could often give piecemeal aid until a family's crisis was over. The most important thing, however, was that the boss was of the people he helped. He and his machine, from one point of view, were the device by which the underprivileged could best confront the unsympathetic establishment. The failure and humiliation that one felt in speaking across a desk to a well-dressed, well-spoken, and well-meaning person did not exist with the ward boss who had grown up in the supplicant's neighborhood, lived in the same houses, played in the same streets, run from the same policemen. He had seen the same depravity, breathed the same air, smelled the same stench in the halls of the same tenements; his parents too had been poor, his family hungry and begging for relief. The boss held out hope, not only because he understood the poor and would help them without embarrassment, but because he symbolized their power to manipulate the distant and alien political establishment.

Modern sociology would call the social complex of the ward a subculture. The settlement people were not far from that conception. "Ward politics," it was observed, "is built up out of racial, religious, industrial affiliations; out of blood kinship; out of childhood associations, youthful camaraderie, general neighborhood sociability. Party regularity is simply the coalescence of all of these." Here is an important truth. For, just as the settlement workers were not dealing with a simple political organization when studying ward politics, charity workers were not investigating mere cases of poverty when observing the poor. Rather, the poor were a whole complex of social relationships, having their own rules and values, almost autonomous although existing within the context of a larger and more familiar social structure. "Ward politics is an amplified scheme of family communism—a modernized clan." Some day, Robert A. Woods said, "it may perhaps become apparent to the historian, looking back, that this clan life in the midst of civilization went with the industrial and social confusion of the time."[35] But Woods was one of the few to see this in his own time.

Perhaps the clearest way to see how alien from the poor the reformer was is to observe his efforts at political reform; it has become commonplace to remark on the distance between the reformer's conception of good government and the needs of the poor. Men who were subject to the caprice of the business cycle coveted the relative permanence of political jobs. Their very ability to secure such jobs, as well as other favors the ward boss could give, depended on a corruption of proper New England government. "The machine politician especially opposed reform measures like that of civil service restrictions and the secret ballot," since such a reform limited his ability to give out jobs and do favors. Thus the respectable Boston lady and gentleman, in their demands for reform, put the slim livelihood of many of the poor in jeopardy, or at least the poor could be made to think so. The best-intended reformer could, therefore, be "looked upon with some of the distrust and fear in which in the Middle Ages the equally truth-loving heretic was viewed—as one who would turn distraught humanity aside from the only way of salvation."[36] The uniqueness of this insight among the reformers attests to the vast human distance that existed between the rich and the poor.

The poor had values and needs different from those the wealthy understood. The middle class held the saloon to be a sink of corruption. Not only did it encourage intemperance by making profit from the moral weakness of its patrons, but it was where the poor wasted money. There was always the vision, sometimes real, of the children and family starving while a man spent his money on beer. The saloon to the poor, however, was a place of adult social relaxation. Often the tradition extended back to the old country, where drinking was rarely considered an evil in itself. Beyond this, after the stultification of the small, stuffy, overcrowded tenement rooms, after the nagging and crying persistence of a wife and numberless children, after the frustrations attendant to economic impotence, the momentary, robust masculinity of the saloon could be a compelling escape.[37] Perhaps Annie Adams Fields was responding to a sense of this need when she worked to establish coffeehouses. Yet the very gentility of her solution indicates the extent of the alienation.

If the "clan" was anything, it was an association for mutual benevolence. The very inability of public and private agencies to meet the needs of the poor in times of emergencies forced the poor to rely on one another, not only in political clubs, but also through informal neighborly assistance. It astonished more than one observer that the poor could uncover sources of aid among their own number even when it appeared that the last drop had been drained. Sometimes the family had a little saving. Small basement stores would give credit. Occasional jobs would turn up. The wife could sometimes find work, even when the husband could not. Children were pressed into employment. Relatives and friends would often be very helpful in supplying food and loaning money. If one owned something of value, there was the pawn shop. In addition to this mutual aid, the help from a charitable society might allow the family to survive.[38] Sometimes the philanthropy of the poor ignored the orthodoxy of respectable benevolence. So it was when a visitor reported "a little white child, motherless, who is living with some colored people."[39] Common suffering could inspire selfless compassion. The family was finally convinced that the child should be given up to the state.

The differences in values of the poor were not merely attitudes that were assumed to achieve political ends. They could not have been merely put on to deceive a do-gooder. The poor man's attitudes were involuntary, formed by the conditions of his life. The labyrinth of alleys through which he ran as a child—rubbish, rotting garbage, lean-to shacks that sheltered people—defined the geography of his world. Humanity pressed together in small, airless tenement rooms —brothers and sisters, other bodies in bed, other arms and legs, the wheeze and stiflement of others' breath—comprised family and intimacy. A world of no secrets. Family and non-family knew all because they heard and saw all. Public water closets, a classroom of a kind: bold instructions for all to read; eyes to watch you come and go; eyes and people to intrude on pubescent privacies. Houses and lives with paper-thin walls, family sounds like the noise of the street: private life a public thoroughfare. Primary instruction was everywhere. How sophisticated about sex these young people must have been! How alien their lives were from Victorian ideals! How difficult it must have been for a respectable woman, like Lillian Clarke, to understand or to be understood![40]

Sometimes failure of communication was the result of blatant collisions of cultures. The charity workers often dealt with people they called foreigners. Immigration was at its peak during these years, and the native American was not sophisticated in ethnology.[41] By the same token it was difficult for foreigners to understand the demands that the benevolent societies made on them. A group of Russian Jews who came to Boston in 1882 must have been confused. Recent refugees from eastern European pogroms, many without funds and unable to speak the language, they appealed to both public and private agencies. The normal machinery of the societies was too awkward to treat their problem, and the conflicting assumptions of the workers and refugees made the charity effort a farce. Communication was an insuperable problem, especially with the Provident's tendency to suspect

fraud; the interviews "had to be carried on through inter-
preters who themselves were Russians, and would naturally
sympathize with their fellow-countrymen; and their veracity
was not above suspicion."[42]

Both state and private agencies were confused. About sixty
of the immigrants were sent to Tewksbury Almshouse to
await the arrival of ships to return them to Europe at the
state's expense. "But the discipline of the Almshouse and
the sagacity of the officials there soon brought to light the
true state of affairs. . . . Some of them were found to be in
possession of considerable sums of money." Most were sent
back to Boston.

The Provident Association then tried to work with the
United Hebrew Benevolent Association, which had not been
anxious to take the cases. The two societies treated these people as they would domestic poor. The Provident demanded
a work test to determine whether or not they were fraudulent. The able-bodied men were invited to come to the
woodyard where they could earn a dollar a day. Only two
appeared. "Their behavior," the Provident concluded, "forcibly illustrates the folly of encouraging any man or any body
of men to expect charity as a matter of course." It is significant, of course, that the Provident Association aided many
of these people and their families. But it is more noteworthy
that they had been expected to understand a charity which
was wholly of an Anglo-Saxon tradition.

The charity worker found the cultural obstacles difficult to
overcome, but the poor had their problems too. Sitting in
her small, hot, disordered kitchen, watching and listening
to the woman who has come to help: Yes, things could be
better if they were kept clean and in good order; but they
never seemed to be clean and in good order no matter how
hard one worked and one was tired—the lady seemed so calm
and neat, everything in place. Yes, perhaps with a little care
the meager fare could be stretched to last longer, but where

did one find time and energy for a little care—the lady had another family to visit before she returned home. Yes, if the older boy went to trade school, he could help in a short time, but the neighbor's boy ran off when she tried to make him help—how could you force a boy to stay? Yes, if the man didn't drink, there would be more money, he could work more regularly, he would stay home more, and he would be less vicious and brutal, but how can you stop a man, except to nag or threaten to leave? Leave? Go where and for what? In those singular instances when a nerve was touched to make her a woman or a human or anybody, it was the man's hand that moved, whether through love or passion or brutality. Self is defined in strange ways; how can you tell it to the little lady who sits across the room fingering her gloves?

Or, to go for charity on Chardon Street, there was the mob. Crowds of dirty people—dirty, unpleasant, ashamed—pressed close in the offices for relief. There was the smell of dirty old clothes that always follows the poor, the stench and must of spittle, and the scraping sounds of feet, coughs, and grumbling. Were they all the same? Was one like another? Did one see himself across the room? Some were real bums. How can one show that he is not a bum when he looks like the rest? How can one appear deserving? The interview—a clean and respectable man behind a desk—so many questions. Get the story straight. Show you're not a bum. The story can't sound like a lie. It must be true, must be the truth. A ticket, food, and fuel for a while anyway. There is warm blood in the cheeks as eyes are passed in the outer room. Hot blood in the cheeks as the policeman watches. The wind fires burning blood in the cheeks on wintry streets outside. There is an emptiness no food can fill as children break bread, won at such a loss. Pray to God that . . . will it have to be? How can one go back again?[43]

Sometimes the voice of a personality broke through the austere records of charitable organizations and the papers

of the reformer so that the reader can sense the poor person
as a real character, a fellow human creature to be contended
with. The voices were rarely heard and never well received.
Annie Adams Fields was a little surprised at the demand for
respect of "my Irish washerwoman who told me she would
not work for *her* [Mrs. Hunt] because *she locked up everything and called her by her Christian name* when she was an
aged woman."[44] Mrs. Emily Tweedy, who was fifty years old
in 1878, found it impossible to remain at the Home for Aged
Colored Women. "She was too active and defiant for such a
place." Mrs. Tweedy "left the Home in the spring, to be
housekeeper for a widower whom she had formerly known."
She was "restless and discontented during the two years she
had been with us, and left without gratitude for the care she
had received." Apparently, Mrs. Tweedy was not yet ready
to retire from life into a home for the aged. She might have
been pleased to learn that the Home's minimum age for inmates was raised on her account.[45]

As long as the reformers saw the poor as merely people
without money or ability or character, they would have difficulty seeing them as individuals at all. Assumptions about the
nature of social and economic change determined the charity
workers' schemes. They believed, first of all that economics
was determined by an immutable natural law. While changes
could be effected by normal adjustment of factors of the economy—capital, rent, and wages—nothing but mischief would
result from tampering. Reformers assumed that the natural
or ideal community was the small one. The modern city,
while inevitable, was regretted. Finally, they believed that the
real need of the common man was a calling, a trade, a skill to
make him independent. Alienation tended to give a special
urgency to the reformers' iteration of these beliefs.

.The belief in the immutability of economic laws caused
endless speculation. The only way to raise wages, and therefore the standard of living, was to increase the capital fund.

But this could be done only by saving. So it became a difficult issue for the charitable societies to decide whether immigration, and the cheap labor it supplied, were good or not.
After all, cheap labor meant low costs and more to invest
and, subsequently, more wages to labor. Immigrants, on the
other hand, used to a lower standard of living, competed un-
fairly with native American workers. Yet immigration restriction was an unnatural tampering with the economy.

There was ambivalence toward immigration control in the
1880s, but there seemed to be no question that the immigrant was to be damned for labor agitation. Labor unrest
was understood to be European inspired and a great damage
and waste of human and economic resources. Since strikes for
higher wages added nothing productive to the economy, they
merely prevented production and used up savings. Like the
political club, unions tended to fragment society.[46]

Organized labor was only grudgingly recognized by Boston's charitable societies. In their maintenance of craft standards, unions were applauded, but when demands were made
for higher wages and shorter hours they were considered disruptive to the economy. It was the free market that should
determine conditions.

The settlement workers, however, were notable exceptions
in their attitude toward organized labor. They tended to see
unions as a means of raising the standard of labor and living
and of organizing power against a collective industry; their
writings are relatively free of legalistic conceptions of economics.[47] But for the rest, unions intruded on the right of
contract and therefore confounded the free market. "It has
been generally recognized that what the employed will take
and the employers give is the only rule to determine wages.
What is best for both parties is freedom of contract in open
market, as well for wages as commodities."[48]

What disturbed most reformers about the labor union was
its usurpation of individual responsibility. The basis of the

American system was the individual's contractual arrangements with others in his society; he succeeded or failed through ability. Thus, it was wrong for outsiders—unions, benevolent societies, or government—to intrude or try forcibly to regulate his life. Indeed, the only hope for amelioration of economic distress was enlightened relations between management and labor, which would come from individual initiative rather than the coercion of government or private organizations. Good works and instances of benevolent capitalism were always applauded. The Paris Exposition of 1867 was not to be the last occasion when prizes were awarded for " 'persons, establishments, or localities which have developed in a remarkable manner, good order and harmony among operatives, and promoted their moral, intellectual and physical well-being in an eminent degree.' "[49]

Economic laws were thought to provide ground rules for community interaction; they were restatements of traditional ideals. The central notion was that the individual was finally responsible for his own welfare. The only mitigating force was Christian benevolence. Economic crises were to be expected; therefore the wise man looked ahead. The solution to personal suffering due to unemployment was "the savings banks, where our large accumulations provide against unexpected disappointment." Worthy characters would find the laws beneficial. "A special blessing attends thrift and economy prompted by regard for dependents, which so often becomes the foundation of competence and wealth." Everyone alike was subject to these laws. Both poor and rich must first look after their families' welfare. Only then might one work in the community interest through private or public benevolence.[50]

Concern about community fragmentation and class alienation was manifest in a theme of nostalgia, the recollection of an earlier, smaller Boston where everyone's condition was known. Doubtless the small community had been ideal; everyone could be observed, the worthy poor attended to and frauds apprehended. The change from small town to city explained to many the difficulties of giving adequate relief to the poor. It justified a charity reform which opposed casual giving. Individualism, thus, pivoted on a conception of the small society that often romanticized town and rural life.

In the early 1870s the city was still talked of as an evil place, and workers were discouraged from leaving the country. It was always assumed that employment was to be found in the country by anyone who would look. And if actual jobs were not plentiful, the country was better for the poor because food was more abundant and living was cheaper. The Industrial Aid Society actually made efforts to encourage farmers to hire by the year, rather than by the season, in order to attract men to the country and prevent seasonal drifts of farm labor to the city. The advantages of the country life over the city life were assumed in the many farm efforts by charitable societies. The Children's Aid Society, for instance, never questioned that training boys to farm in the 1880s and 1890s would be of value to them. The farms were finally given up with great reluctance; the city had come too close to West Newton, the electric cars were almost to the door. A new farm, farther away, seemed unreasonable because of expense. This sentiment for country life was responsible for the temporary experiments in city farming in 1893. It also justified the removal of some of the poor from Boston, individually and in families.[51]

This nostalgia for the smaller, simpler community was, in part, a recognition of the complexities of urban life in the late nineteenth century. It was also a resistance to some of the imperatives of an industrial age. After all, large urban populations, undifferentiated and often unemployed, were important to industry at the particular stage of development it had reached. Existing social-service agencies were not designed to meet the problems that such labor pools presented. Confronting the city's growth, the heterogeneity and size of its lower classes, charitable societies became conscious of their impotence to control the community. It is not surprising that they recalled earlier times when the city was small enough that traditional ideals could pervade it, and when most people could be observed and understood. Significantly, the keystone of charity reform was the small district governed by voluntary visitors and paid agents.

The benevolent societies also regretted the difficulty that men found in gaining trades. The passing of the apprentice system had been one of the early concerns of the Industrial Aid Society, which thought the demise due to the false pride of parents and the low pay and status of mechanical labor. More likely, the decline of the small craftsman and the apprentice system was another result of the industrial revolution. The factory system found less need for skilled craftsmen of the kind produced under journeymen and masters. The building trades and other craft unions developed their own methods of training and job control. The dissatisfaction that was expressed throughout the period, however, was not so much that a particular system had vanished, but that no method of producing craftsmen which would satisfactorily merge labor and capital had taken its place.[52]

Benevolent individuals worked hard in the last decades of the century to establish vocational-training programs. They insisted that by giving young people a skill the greatest good would be accomplished. Mrs. Augustus Hemenway's experiments and subsidies of public-school classes, and the great number of industrial schools started during the period, illustrate this general concern. Manual training (as opposed to vocational training) also had supporters. It seemed that all schools and institutions were experimenting with teaching children to work with their hands. Children, it was felt, had to be convinced that they could be proud of a skill, that manual labor was not degrading. Some of the skills that were taught (domestic work, for instance) were of questionable value. Yet the important thing, it seemed, was to have a trade. The argument for it was very pragmatic. Classical education was brought under attack; John Dewey was, in part, anticipated.[53]

With the growing community fragmentation—the dislodgement of traditional ideals—men and women working in charitable organizations struggled to maintain control over the morals of the city. Their efforts were not merely pronouncements and publications. But whenever the issues of vagrancy, begging, free soup, saloons (temperance), or control of the police were discussed by the City Council, charitable organizations would be represented to advance their position. Indeed, much of the pressure for reform in these matters was exerted by philanthropic societies.

From their beginning, benevolent organizations had insisted on control of beggars and tramps. At first their plans were merely to establish workhouses so that vagrants would be separated from both criminals in the jails and the virtuous poor in almshouses. Their plans were later elaborated into schemes for uplift and education of the tramp class. But begging was still growing in 1885. The societies were unhappy that they had so little control over the problem. Their literature persuaded against indiscriminate almsgiving; people were encouraged to report beggars for investigation. The Industrial Aid Society began to put pressure on the city to control the conditions at the Wayfarer's Lodge. And the Society for the Prevention of Cruelty to Children got a law passed which prohibited children from peddling and begging; the law was generally applauded by the benevolent societies.[54]

The objections to free soup were essentially two: it was given by the police, who were not equipped to determine the need of the poor, and "daily distributions of public relief has a strong tendency to lower the tone and destroy the self-reliance of many of those who avail themselves of it." The latter objection rested on the charity reformers' bias against outdoor relief of any kind, assuming the worthy poor's disinclination to accept such relief anyway; free soup attracted the marginal poor and beggars. In their criticism of the police distribution, however, the societies attacked an irresponsibility which allowed politics to influence police doles as it had their granting of liquor licenses.[55]

The pressure exerted by the charitable societies to reform or remove the Boston police commissioners in 1881 and 1882 reflects their anxiety about community control. Far back into the 1850s the Boston police had been authorized to aid and support the charitable societies and their visitors.[56] There was no complaint against the police's cooperation in small matters concerning visiting the poor. The police tended to be connected with the local political clubs, however, and were not especially sympathetic to the reformers. Removing the police commissioners became the great cause in the early 1880s. Annie Adams Fields wrote to Governor Long that she would like to see the police commissioners appointed by the state, an obvious effort to remove them from local politics. "Our work for the poor in Boston," she claimed, "is almost neutralized by the absence of help from the very source where we should look for it."[57]

Continual pressure by reformers caused the removal of the police commissioners the following year. This act was applauded by Robert Treat Paine. He left no doubt that he expected the police to be an arm of the charitable societies. Paine saw the police as more than the coercive agency of the community; they should be an active force for the good. The commissioners had to be able to infuse the proper spirit into the men. Ideally, Paine wrote, the police "can exercise a real power to prevent intoxication & all the misery, the family broils & fights, the neglect of children & the crowding of jails &c which follow from intoxication." Further, Paine held, the police could prevent crime. Their job was not "merely to arrest criminals—but to prevent a multitude of near crimes & especially children becoming criminals."[58]

The police issue was another indication of the reformers' struggle against ward politics.[59] In 1883 the reformer could congratulate himself on the defeat of Benjamin Butler and, therefore, the defeat of the Irish political machine, but it was only a matter of time before the Irish would win altogether. "We have in Massachusetts," said one observer, "the penalty of our hospitality. We have thrown the State open to the Irish, and like the snake in the fable, they reward us by a Butler bite. I can only hope that their eyes may be opened before long."[60]

The loss of political power and social influence—estrangement within their home—caused respectable Bostonians considerable anxiety. Their charitable effort became a means of asserting control. The admitted primary objective of private charity in the last half of the nineteenth century was to improve the poor; uplift was a kind of management. For this reform was meant to be moral as well as physical. Indeed, few organizations considered it possible to better the physical state of a man; one could only infuse in him spirit and discipline and train him to self-sufficiency. The charity reformer understood charity to be a sufficient lever to achieve this end, only if it was used sparingly and with intelligence. The great discovery of the nineteenth century, as R. H. Tawney observed, was that relief might be administered not merely to relieve, but also to deter.[61] But the outlet of relief had to be under the most strict control. No police officer or small politician could be allowed to give aid at his own discretion.

While the charity reformer wanted to limit public relief, he never argued against public aid altogether. Nor did he reject the poor as socially unfit, as did the Social Darwinists. Rather, he was perfectly pleased to aid the worthy poor as long as the relief was temporary and made the poor man better able to care for himself.

It is, at first, surprising that in an age dominated by Darwinism the literature of the Boston charities should show little sign of its influence. Most reformers considered society to be an organism which innocent tampering could disrupt. But they believed that a sophisticated social science could instruct the social engineer how best to reform. Still, they leaned to individual reform and uplift as the solution to most social ills. While neither Darwin nor Sumner is much mentioned in the literature, it becomes apparent that there are interesting similarities between the charity reformer's "worthy poor" and William Graham Sumner's "Forgotten Man."[62]

The charity workers wrote most about the unworthy poor and only suggested their ideal man. The unworthy cases were "indolent, and do not wish to work if they can live without it." As this characteristic was deplored, "habits of industry, of perseverance, and of prudence"[63] could well stand throughout the period for the primary characteristics of the worthy poor. The ideal poor man was the responsible head of a family and a church member, constant in his observances. He was not subject to passion; thus he was temperate in all things. He was reluctant to ask for assistance from anyone outside his immediate family; he would depend on the State only as a final resort, if ever, and private assistance had to be forced on him as a means of keeping his family alive. He was interested in self-improvement and diligence to rise in social and economic status. He was disinterestedly involved in politics, never using government as a means to achieve personal ends. Finally, and perhaps most important, he had to have a calling, a skill or trade or enterprise through which he gained his livelihood and to which he gave his energy. It did not matter if it was a humble occupation; what did matter was that he was devoted to its performance. Those societies which aided the poor "who had seen better times" believed that their cases were guaranteed to be worthy because of an affluent or respectable history.[64]

The ideals that are expressed in this composite description of a worthy man were not peculiar to charity reformers. When Frederick Bushée attempted to describe the American ideals to which the immigrant must aspire, he assumed these criteria. He judged, without much perception and with a great deal of prejudice, the ethnic groups of the South End by these standards. And, while William Graham Sumner never clearly defined his "Forgotten Man," his essays unquestionably suggest that his ideal man personified these characteristics.[65] The similarity does not end here. Surely, such simple virtues as industry, frugality, temperance, fidelity to family and to God, and moderate ambitions go deeper in the American heritage than the nineteenth century. Of course, one finds them applauded by Benjamin Franklin. Max Weber and R. H. Tawney have portrayed these ideals, at least as they pertain to enterprise, as the Protestant ethic.[66]

It is more than a coincidence that private persons, engaged in philanthropic works, would insist on holding up these ideals to the poor, while, at the same time, these identical standards would measure the extent of the immigrant's assimilation and judge the fitness of man to survive. It was all one ethical standard, like Mrs. Field's self-perfection, finding its roots in Puritanism and Transcendental idealism. Indeed, it would appear that the Protestant ethic had been assumed by Puritans in the first instant.

It is not surprising that private charity in the late nineteenth century should adopt a religious ethic as its norm for judging human behavior. The charity-reform movement grew out of religious activity to begin with. To say that charities enunciated a Protestant ethic is merely to describe in a different way the secularization of Protestantism. Seen from one point of view the religious impulse was losing to a social ethic, while from the other viewpoint it would appear that social institutions had vestiges of religious demands. Each view shows a different facet of the same condition.

That the Protestant church was losing its power in the community after 1870 seemed to be a fact. Francis G. Peabody's department of social ethics at Harvard is evidence that the ministry failed to appeal to socially minded young men. Peabody himself claimed that his program was meant to attract students who formerly would have gone into the Divinity School. Charles W. Birtwell said much the same thing when he appealed to young men to enter social work. Birtwell wanted dedicated young men who might have been ministers in former years. So, too, with the social emphasis of the program at the Phillips Brooks House at Harvard. All this attests to the fact that the ministry was no longer the profession for a man who wanted to be effective in improving society. Social work was seen, at least in its early years, as the new social ministry.[67]

Parallels with an earlier age are tempting. Of course they are too easy and too simple to give a precise truth. Nevertheless, if we look at the charity worker in 1900 as the secular equivalent of William Ellery Channing's and Joseph Tuckerman's minister-at-large, we will have some flavor of the truth. And we can go further, for theology had its later secular equivalents. The Calvinistic tone of William Graham Sumner holding to his fit remnant, damning the rest to their ditch, has been remarked by others.[68] In contrast to this secular orthodoxy, the liberal charity reformer anticipated redemption and worked to save the poor from the hell of pauperism. Thus, private charity in the late nineteenth century was one of many transformations of a traditional ethic. The charity worker used his organizations to guarantee the moral fabric in a community which seemed to be raveling in diversity.

NOTES

1. For biographical data on Mrs. Fields see *Dictionary of American Biography*, ed. Allan Johnson and Dumas Malone (New York, 1931), IV, 377–378; Associated Charities, *Reports*, XXXVI (1915) 10–11; Mark A. DeW. Howe, *Memories of a Hostess* (Boston, 1922); Henry James, *The*

American Scene (New York, 1907), esp. Chs. 1 and 7; Henry James, "Mr. and Mrs. James T. Fields," *Atlantic Monthly,* CXVI (July 1915), 21–31; Boston *Transcript,* January 5, 6, 1915, as well as her papers in Houghton and MHS. For Charles R. Codman: The Harvard Class of 1849, files in the Archives of Harvard University; Boston *Transcript,* October 5, 1918; and the Codman papers at the MHS.

2. Fields, Diary, "Easter Sunday," April 6, 1873.

3. Ibid., [January], 1874.

4. Ibid., December 13, 1871; July 16, 1872.

5. Lillian Clarke, "Diaries" among the papers of James Freeman Clarke at Houghton Library.

6. Harvard College. "Faculty Record," XIII, 19, 24, 31, 70–71, 107, 108, 111, 118, 121, 174, 201, 207, 273, 288, 296, 297, 322; Harvard Class of 1849, "Class Book," 149–150; Notebook of James Holden Lander among the papers of the Class of 1849. All of these records are to be found in Harvard University Archives.

7. Boston *Transcript,* October 5, 1918.

8. Fields, Miscellaneous Papers, MHS, dated 1875; Diary, n.d., ca. Easter, 1875.

9. Letter from Francis E. Parker to S. G. Ward, October 2, 1872; letters from Francis E. Parker to S. G. Ward, June 17, 1881, and July 3, 1881, Parker papers, Houghton.

10. Letter from Francis E. Parker to S. G. Ward, December 31, 1873, Houghton. It is interesting to note that Mrs. Fields hated the frivolousness of New York society, and she became physically ill whenever she accompanied her husband there on his lecture circuit (see Diary, 1875–76).

11. Fields, Diary, June 15, 1871; August 15, 1871; May 15, 1871.

12. Codman, Miscellaneous papers, dated November 26, 1889, MHS; Augustus Mongredien, *On the Displacement of Labour and Capital* (London, 1886) is the pamphlet Codman referred to.

13. Ibid.

14. Codman, Draft of letter to Howard O. Sturgis, n.d., among the Codman papers, MHS; the novel in question is H. O. Sturgis, *All that Was Possible* (London, 1896).

15. Fields, Diary, April 6, 1873.

16. Ibid., June 11, 1874.

17. Ibid., January 2, 1871; Mrs. Fields quotes the French: "Ne nous laison pas abattre pourtant, il faut moins pour se résigner à l'indigence quand on sent avec passion la vue du soleil, des arbres, de la douce lumière et la croyance profonde de revoir les aimés que l'on pleure." The passage may be found in C. A. Sainte-Beuve, *Madame Desbordes-Valmore, Sa Vie et sa Correspondance* (Paris, 1870). 141.

18. Fields, Diary, is filled with references to small works like this. There are many comments on coffee houses; note particularly: November 12, 24, 1870; November 13, 1871; March 22 and November 30, 1872.

19. Letter from Annie Adams Fields to Otis Norcross, November 26,

1872, MHS, approval by William Gray written at the bottom.

20. Barbara Miller Solomon, *Ancestors and Immigrants* (Cambridge, Mass., 1956), Chs. 1–3, discusses this estrangement.

21. Fields, Diary, July 9, 1873.

22. Ibid., July 18, 1874.

23. Ibid., July 9, 1873.

24. Ibid., April 5, 1875.

25. Ibid., May 7, 1875.

26. Ibid., May 1, 1872.

27. Ibid., September 25, 1876.

28. Ibid., n.d., ca. July 20, 1874.

29. Ibid., July 31, 1874.

30. Fields, Miscellaneous papers, "Notes on travels to England," ca. 1900, p. 43 (MHS).

31. Ibid., "September 6," p. 3; for Mrs. Fields's later views on charity see her *How to Help the Poor* (Boston, 1883), esp. Chs. 4 and 6.

32. Codicil to the last will and testament of Annie Adams Fields, typescript copy among Fields's papers, Houghton.

33. Last Will and Testament of Annie Adams Fields, typescript copy, pp. 4–5, Fields's papers, Houghton. Mr. Fields was educated in the Portsmouth, N.H., public schools and was too poor to attend college (*Dictionary of American Biography*, IV, 378).

34. Woods, *Americans*, 174–175; see Davis, *Spearheads For Reform*, for settlement workers' more sophisticated understanding of the conditions and resources of the urban poor.

35. Ibid., 149–150.

36. Ibid., 149, 154. Woods, *Americans*, is rich in sharp observations about the "clan"; see esp. Chs. 6, 7, 11, 12. See also Woods, *City*, Chs. 6, 11.

37. Woods, *City*, 288–292.

38. Woods, *Americans*, 129, 135; *City*, 137n, 144–145.

39. Instructive District Nurses, Records of the Meeting of Managers, June 29, 1892.

40. For descriptions of living conditions see Woods, *Americans*, 99–100 218–219; Woods, *City*, 31, 33–34; *Lend A Hand*, I (December 1886), 741–743; Albert Benedict Wolfe, *The Lodging House Problem in Boston* (Boston, 1906), esp. Ch. 13; for tenement and slum housing, but in New York, see James Ford et al., *Slums and Housing* (Cambridge, Mass., 1936).

41. Woods, *Americans*, Ch. 3, and Woods, *City*, Ch. 3, for particularly ignorant observations by the sociologist Frederick A. Bushée.

42. Provident, *Report*, XXXII (1883), 8–10, gives a complete account from one point of view; also Provident, "Records," January 11, 1883.

43. Conditions at the Charity Building were so bad that directors continually asked to move or make other changes: Provident *Report*, XLIII (1894), 7–8; "Records," April 13, 1877, and March 10, 1887; IAS, "Records," April 15, 1891; "Executive Committee Report," February 4, 1885.

44. Fields, Diary, May 21, 1875, Mrs. Fields's emphasis.

45. Boston Home for Aged Colored Women, *Report*, XIX (1878), 6; XX (1879), 7.

46. IAS, *Report*, LI (1886), 13-15; LII (1887), 6-10, currency question discussed, favors some silver (pp. 8-9); but see letter from Henry P. Kidder to W. W. Clapp, February 12, 1883, Kidder papers, Houghton. For argument supporting the importation of Chinese and Negroes for domestics see SPS, *Report*, XXXI (1866), 14-15; XXIV (1869), 13-15; IAS, *Report*, XXXV (1870), 15-16.

47. Woods, *Americans*, 376, and *City*, 282; Denison House, Report (1895), 3-4; Davis, *Spearheads For Reform*, Ch. 6.

48. IAS, *Report*, LII (1887), 6.

49. Letter from Samuel Eliot to Caroline H. Dall, December 2, 1866, Samuel Eliot papers, MHS; see also *Lend A Hand*, I (September 1886), 509-511. This view is common in the literature; see Edward Everett Hale's utopian works.

50. IAS, *Report*, LII (1887), 8; Fatherless and Widow's Society, *Report*, LXVI (1883), 3-4, for an interesting statement of this view with religious emphasis.

51. Workers should stay in country, IAS, *Report*, XXXVIII (1873), 11-12; rural life cheaper, *Lend A Hand*, I (April 1886), 192; attempt to influence farmers, IAS, *Report*, XLV (1880), 3-4; urban encroachment on farm, CAS, *Report*, XXXIII (1896), 21, and XXXV (1899), 11; farm plans, IAS, *Report*, LX (1895), 6-7 (see also "Records," April 20, 1898); removals from city, IAS, *Report*, XXXIX (1874), 4-5, and XLII (1897), 5-6. For an interesting view on the value of the farm see CAS, *Report*, VIII (1872), 5-6, and Robert Treat Paine, "Address to the Children's Aid Society, March 24, 1890," among the papers of the Children's Aid Association.

52. SPP, *Report*, XXXIII (1868), 10-11, and XXXIV (1869), 15-16; IAS, *Report*, XLV (1880), 13-15, and XLVI (1881), 7-8; CAS, *Report*, XXII (1886), 6-7; letter from Edward Everett Hale to Thomas W. Higginson, December 4, 1887, Hale papers, Houghton.

53. "Saving Boys and Girls," Boston *Evening Transcript*, January 17, 1891; CAS, *Report*, XXVI (1890), 13, and XXVII (1891), 24-25; *Lend A Hand* has a regular column by Lucretia P. Hale, "Walks in Boston Schools," which discusses these matters. See Ch. 5, above, for a discussion of the establishment of trades schools.

54. SPP, *Report*, XXII (1857), 15; IAS, *Report*, XL (1877), 10-12, and "Executive Committee Report" February 7, March 7, April 4, 1898, and February 4, 1901; Provident, *Report*, XXXIV (1885), 10-11.

55. Provident, *Report*, XXXIII (1884), 9-10, and "Records," December 8, 1893; for criticism of police and liquor licenses and insistence on lobbying at the State House, see IAS, "Executive Committee Report," December 9, 1901; but the minutes of the Boston City Council and City Documents show these debates; Roger Lane, *Policing the City of Boston, 1822-1865* (Cambridge, Mass., 1967).

56. Provident, "Records," May 5, 1853.

57. Letter from Annie Adams Fields to Governor Long, February 21, 1881, Fields's papers, MHS.

58. Letter from Robert Treat Paine to Samuel A. Green, April 6, 1882, Paine papers, MHS.

59. Woods, *City*, Ch. 6.

60. Letter from Samuel Eliot to Caroline H. Dall, November 13, [1883,] Dall papers, MHS; for similar comment on Butler see letter from Franklin Sanborn to Caroline H. Dall, October 29, 1883, Dall papers, MHS.

61. R. H. Tawney, *Religion and the Rise of Capitalism* (New York, 1962), 271.

62. A notable exception is an article which fuses the social organism concept and the iron law of wages: J. G. Brooks, "Social Questions," *Lend A Hand*, I (January 1886), 10–13.

63. IAS, *Report*, XXXIX (1874), 7.

64. Howard Benevolent Society, *Report*, LXX (1882), 6–8, for an assertion of this belief; LXXXI (1893), 8, aid is forced on a worthy case. Similar statements may be found throughout this Society's *Reports* and those of the Fatherless and Widow's Society and the Home for Aged Men—all established to assist "Americans" who had seen better times.

65. Frederick A. Bushée, "The Invading Host," Ch. 3 in Woods, *City*, 40–70; William Graham Sumner, "The Forgotten Man," in *Essays of William Graham Sumner*, ed. A. G. Keller and M. R. Davie (New Haven, 1934), I, 466–496; Sumner, *What Social Classes Owe to Each Other* (New York, 1920), passim.

66. Max Weber, *The Protestant Ethic, and the Spirit of Capitalism*, trans. Talcott Parsons (New York, 1958), Ch. 2; Tawney, *Rise of Capitalism*, Ch. 4.

67. See Ch. 4, above.

68. Richard Hofstadter, *Social Darwinism in American Thought* (New York, 1959), 51, has already noted Sumner's tone of orthodoxy.

8

Epilogue

WE should not be deceived. Although charity reformers, in becoming social workers, took on the secular guise of science, they merely masked a deep moralism. The assumption that poverty was a fault of character has persisted in welfare and relief programs into our time. In time, the language was to change, pauper and unworthy poor would no longer be explicit accusations. But the case worker's eligibility criteria implied these concepts, nonetheless. Sentiment, what the reformers had hoped to expunge from philanthropy, actually seemed to disappear amidst system and case records. But, in this, the reformers were victims of self-deception. While asserting traditional morality and fusing it to a belief in automatic progress, they had abandoned the anguished Puritan conscience. Morals, without ultimate, personal obligation became moralism and sentiment, regardless of harsh or antiseptic tone. Their sentimentality was nostalgic rather than humanitarian. Was it not narcissism rather than philanthropy that beckoned the backward glances to the idealized village and prescribed as the palliate to the poor mimicking one's own good character?

Whatever the pretense, moralism and sentimentality were part of the legacy that the Charity Organization Movement left to social work. The professionals were most successful when they mastered some specific skill with which to serve their cases. Roy Lubove has shown this with psychiatric social workers. We have seen something of this as children's services matured to utilize specific skills to remedy particular ills. This same professional success through the application of special training can be seen in the effectiveness of public health nurses as they participate in the broad spectrum of activities called social work. But, clearly, where the social-work enterprise has been most a failure is in what the charity reformers were most anxious about, relief and welfare for the impoverished.

The failure, no doubt, stands to reason. After all, the reformers were nowhere more confused than where they attempted to apply their moral strictures and dogma to the victims of urban and industrial crises. Their idea that alms to those in desperate need could only be a temporary relief— improvement and uplift coming through caseworkers' aid— has become a fiction of the mid-twentieth century. Few cities would claim that their welfare programs and their aid to dependent children do more than prevent starvation.

The charity reformers' legacy to the welfare system heightens the irony. For, with all of the visiting, the record keeping, the search for eligibility, and the pretense of remedial care, what William Ellery Channing, Joseph Tuckerman, Thomas Chalmers, and all of their heirs would have called pauperism has become the general condition of the poor: men, women, and children wholly dependent on the alms of welfare, and, in fact, demanding it as a right.

Those who would read Channing's *The Obligation of a City* today would find its warnings and anxieties remarkably contemporary. The ligaments of Christian obligation have long since failed to maintain the tension of materialism and spiritualism within the community. He had warned that large cities could become two nations, knowing little of one another—the rich and the poor. He had urged that the greatest thing in a city was man himself, not property, not material progress. The happy city had to know that man was worth more than all the wealth and buildings and show. If society "will not use its prosperity," Channing asserted, "to save the ignorant and poor from the blackest vice, if it will even quicken vice by its selfishness and luxury, its worship of wealth, its scorn of human nature, then it must suffer, and deserves to suffeɪ, from crime." Man had a social and moral obligation to his brothers. To Channing, and his generation, the common weal (the community) was a covenant which obliged the rich as well as the poor, testing the character of both. To the later charity reformers, however, only the character of the poor was in doubt. They never sought to test the worthy rich and the worthy community.

The charity reformers' moralism and self-indulgent sentimentality deflected them from seeing the poor as adult men and women. Rather, they were a problem to be acted on, dealt with, reformed, and uplifted. Having such a view, and accepting conventional concepts of political economy, the reformers were unable to see the simple truth that has struck some present-day social thinkers: the problem with the poor is that they have no money. Mr. Homos, Howells' visitor from Altruria, saw it this way. But the implications of that insight are more radical than the genteel charity reformers could have dared to accept. For that would have obliged them to consider ways of distributing the society's wealth so that humanity would not be dishonored by inequity. That is the citadel that any successful war on poverty must control.

Bibliography

Primary Sources

GOVERNMENT DOCUMENTS

Federal

U.S. Treasury Department, Bureau of Statistics. *Statistical Abstract of the United States.* I–V (1878–1882).

State

Commonwealth of Massachusetts, Commission on Public and Charitable Interests and Institutions. *Report.* Boston, 1897.

———. Joint Standing Committee on Public and Charitable Institutions. *Report on the State Almshouse at Tewksbury.* House Document No. 300. 2 vols. Boston, 1883.

———. Commission on Public Charities. *Report.* Public Document No. 38. Boston, 1878.

———. *Labor Bulletin.* 1897–1900.

Massachusetts Board to Investigate the Subject of the Unemployed. *Report.* House Document No. 50. Boston, 1895.

Massachusetts Bureau of the Statistics of Labor. *Reports.* 1869–1900.

Massachusetts State Board of Charities. *Annual Reports.*

City

Boston Overseers of the Poor. *Annual Reports.* 1865–1900.

MANUSCRIPTS

The following list of names is selected from a larger group whose papers were systematically searched at Houghton, Harvard University, and the Massachusetts Historical Society. The original list was compiled because of frequency within benevolent societies' reports. The following list represents those collections of papers that contributed to this study. For convenience (H) and (MHS) will abbreviate Houghton and Massachusetts Historical Society respectively.

Baldwin, William H. (H, MHS).

Brimmer, Martin (H, MHS).

Clarke, James Freeman (H) Diaries of Lillian Clarke.

Codman, Charles R. (MHS).

Eliot, Samuel, (H, MHS).

Fields, Mrs. James T. (Annie Adams) (H, MHS).

Hale, Edward Everett (H, MHS).

Kidder, Henry P. (H).

Norcross, Otis (MHS).

Paine, Robert Treat (MHS, H).

Parker, Francis (H).

Thayer, Nathaniel (H, MHS).

Warren, John Collins (H, MHS).

Winthrop, Robert C. (MHS).

The manuscript records of meetings and other papers of the following organizations are in the offices of the Boston Children's Service Association.

Boston Children's Aid Society

Boston Children's Friend Society

Female Asylum

Gwynne Temporary Home

North End Mission

The manuscript records of meetings and other papers of the following organizations are in the offices of the Boston Family Service Association.

The Associated Charities

The Boston Provident Society

The Industrial Aid Society (Society for the Prevention of Pauperism before 1870)

The papers of the Instructive District Nurses' Association are to be found in the offices of the Boston Visiting Nurses' Association. Harvard University Archives maintains files of mixed published and manuscript material on students and officers. Of particular interest to this study are the class reports of the classes of 1849 and 1885, Charles Codman's and Charles Birtwell's respectively. The Archives' Quinquennial files relating to Sherman C. Kingsley and Francis G. Peabody were also used.

PUBLICATIONS

The annual reports and other publications of the following organizations were studied throughout the period under investigation. This list is selected from a larger list of organizations.

Boston Children's Aid Society

Boston Children's Friend Society

Boston Dispensary

Boston Fatherless and Widows' Society

Boston Female Asylum. *Reminiscences of the Boston Female Orphan Asylum.* Boston, 1844.

———. *One Hundred Years of Work in Boston.* 1919. Published under the new name of the society: "Boston Society for the Care of Girls."

Boston Lying-In Hospital

Boston Port and Seamen's Aid Society

Boston Provident Society

Boston Young Men's Christian Association

Boston Young Men's Christian Union

Channing Home in Boston

Children's Mission to the Children of the Destitute

City Missionary Society

Committee of Delegates from the Benevolent Societies of Boston *Report.* Boston, 1834.

Cooperative Society of Visitors

Denison House
Ellis Memorial and Eldridge House
Elizabeth Peabody House Association
Farm and Trades School at Thompson's Island
Home for Aged Colored Women
Home for Aged Men
Howard Benevolent Society
Industrial Aid Society (Society for the Prevention of Pauperism)
Industrial School for Crippled and Deformed Children
Instructive District Nurses' Association
Massachusetts Association of Relief Officers
Massachusetts General Hospital
Massachusetts Society for the Prevention of Cruelty to Children
National Conference on Charities and Corrections. *Proceedings.*
New England Home for Little Wanderers
New England Hospital for Women and Children
New England Watch and Ward Society
Norfolk House Center
North Bennet Street Industrial School
North End Industrial Home
South End House
Washingtonian Hospital

NEWSPAPERS AND MAGAZINES

The Boston *Transcript* and the *Advertiser* were used for obituaries and general reference. The following magazines were studied systematically.

Charities Review. 1892–1900.
Lend A Hand. 1886–1890.
North End Mission Magazine. January 1872–January 1875.

BOOKS BY CONTEMPORARIES

Banks, Louis A. *White Slaves; or The Oppression of the Worthy Poor.* Boston, 1892.
Bartol, Cyrus A. *Influence of the Minister at Large in the City of Boston.* Boston, 1892.

Brace, Charles L. *The Best Method of Disposing of Our Pauper and Vagrant Children.* New York, 1859.

Brooks, Phillips. *Christian Charity.* New York, 1911.

———. *The Duty of the Christian Businessman.* Boston [1893].

Cabot, Richard C. *Foregrounds and Backgrounds in Work for the Sick.* Boston, 1906.

Chalmers, Thomas. *The Works of Thomas Chalmers.* 25 vols. Glasgow, 1836–1842.

Channing, William Ellery. *The Obligation of a City.* Glasgow, 1841.

Damon, S[amuel] C. *Report on Charitable Work, 1869–1870.* Boston, 1870.

Fields, Annie Adams. *How to Help the Poor.* Boston, 1883.

Gérando, Joseph Marie de. *The Visitor of the Poor.* "Translated by a Lady of Boston." 2d. ed. Boston, 1833.

Gurteen, S. Humphreys. *A Handbook of Charity Organization.* Buffalo, 1882.

Hale, Edward Everett. *The Duty of the Church in Cities.* Boston, 1878.

[———]. *The First True Gentleman; a Study in the Human Nature of Our Lord.* Boston, 1907.

———. *The Five Great Duties of the Twentieth Century.* Boston, 1901.

———. *How They Lived in Hampton.* Boston, 1888.

———. *If Jesus Came to Boston.* Boston, 1895.

———. *"We, the People."* New York, 1903.

———. *What Career?* Boston, 1878.

———. *Workingmen's Homes.* Boston, 1874.

Hale, Edward Everett, Jr., ed. *The Life and Letters of Edward Everett Hale.* 2 vols. Boston, 1917.

Kellogg, Charles D. *History of Charity Organization in the United States.* Chicago, 1893.

Lincoln, Alice N. *Concerning the Management of Tenement Houses.* Boston, 1887.

Lowell, Josephine Shaw. *Public Relief and Private Charity.* New York, 1884.

Paine, Robert Treat. *Charity Organization.* Boston, 1879.

———. *Co-operative Banks.* Boston, 1880.

———. *The Empire of Charity Established by the Revolution of this Century.* Boston, 1895.

———. *Homes for the People*. Boston, 1882.

———. *Housing Conditions in Boston*. Boston, 1902.

———. *How to Repress Pauperism and Street Begging*. New York, 1883.

———. *The Inspiration of Charity*. Boston, 1905.

———. *Pauperism in Great Cities*. n.p., [1893].

———. *The Relations Between the Church and the Associated Charities*. Boston, 1897.

———. *The Work of Volunteer Visitors of the Associated Charities*. Boston, 1880.

Prevy, C. E. *Economic Aspects of Charity Organization*. Philadelphia, 1899.

Richmond, Mary E. *Friendly Visiting among the Poor*. New York, 1918.

———. *The Long View, Papers and Addresses by Mary Richmond*. Edited by Joanna C. Colcord. New York, 1930.

———. *What is Social Case Work?* New York, 1922.

Sanborn, Franklin B. *The Public Charity of Massachusetts During the Century Ending January 1, 1876*. Boston, 1876.

Spencer, Anna Garlin and Charles W. Birtwell. *The Care of Dependent, Neglected and Wayward Children*. Chicago, 1893.

Sprague, Henry H. *A Brief History of the Massachusetts Charitable Fire Society*. Boston, 1893.

Stedman, Henry R. *The Family System as an Accessory Provision for Our Insane Poor*. n.p., 1884.

Tuckerman, Joseph. *A Letter on the Principles of the Mission-Enterprise*. Boston, 1831.

———. *The Principles and Results of the Ministry-at-Large in Boston*. Boston, 1838.

Ufford, Walter S. *Fresh Air Charity in the United States*. New York, 1897.

Walker, Francis A. *A Plea for Industrial Education in the Public Schools*. Boston, 1887.

Woods, Robert A. *Americans in Process*. Boston, 1902.

———. *The City Wilderness*. Boston, 1898.

———. *Social Work: a New Profession*. New York, 1906.

Wright, J. H. *Thoughts and Experiences of a Charity-Organizationist*. London, 1878.

ARTICLES BY CONTEMPORARIES

Bushée, Frederick, "Ethnic Factors in the Population of Boston," *Publication of the American Economic Association.* 3d Series IV (March, 1903), pp. 299–477.

Closson, Carlos C., "The Unemployed in American Cities," *The Quarterly Journal of Economics,* VIII (1894), pp. 168–217, 257–260, 453–477, and 499–502.

[Coolidge, G.] "The Charities of Boston," *The Boston Almanac,* XXXVI (1871).

Dudley, Helena S., "Relief Work Carried on in the Wells Memorial Institute," American Academy of Political and Social Science, *Annals,* V (November 1894), pp. 377–397.

Hale, Edward Everett, "Higher Life of Boston," *Outlook,* LIII (March 28, 1896), pp. 554–560.

Ingersoll, Robert J., "The Three Philanthropists," *North American Review,* CLIII (December 1891), pp. 661–671.

Lincoln, Alice N., "Some Ways of Benefiting a City—the Poor of Boston," *Municipal Affairs,* II (September 1898), pp. 483–492.

Maurice, C. E., "The Clergy and Charitable Relief," *Macmillan's,* XXXVI (June 1877), pp. 168–171.

"Out-Door Parish Relief," *The Westminister Review,* CI (April 1874), pp. 323–335.

"Philanthropy in America and in Europe," *The Nation,* IV (April 18, 1867), pp. 309–310.

"Public and Private Charities in Boston," *The North American Review,* LXI (July 1845), pp. 135–159.

"The Relief of the Unemployed in the United States During the Winter of 1893–1894," *Journal of Social Science,* XXXII (1894), pp. 1–51.

Synnot, Henrietta L., "Institutions and Their Inmates," *Contemporary Review,* XXVI (August 1875), pp. 487–504.

Willard, Ashton R. "The Rindge Gifts to Cambridge," *New England Magazine,* new series III (February 1891), pp. 761–778.

Secondary Sources

BOOKS

Beard, Mary. *Instructive District Nursing Association: A Review.* Boston, 1921.

Bliss, W. D. P. *The Encyclopedia of Social Reform.* New York, 1897.

Bremner, Robert H. *American Philanthropy.* Chicago, 1960.

———. *From the Depths.* New York, 1956.

Brewer, John M. *History of Vocational Guidance.* New York, 1919.

Bruno, Frank J. *Trends in Social Work as Reflected in the Proceedings of the National Conference on Charities and Corrections, 1874–1946.* New York, 1957.

Christmas, Earl. *The House of Goodwill.* Boston, 1924.

Crawford, Mary Caroline. *Famous Families of Massachusetts.* 2 vols. Boston, 1930.

Davis, Allen F. *Spearheads For Reform.* New York, 1967.

Devine, Edward T. *When Social Work Was Young.* New York, 1939.

Douglass, Harlan P. *The Protestant Church as a Social Institution.* New York, 1935.

Feder, Leah Hannah. *Unemployment Relief in Periods of Depression.* New York, 1936.

Ford, James, et al. *Slums and Housing with Special Reference to New York City.* 2 vols. Cambridge, Massachusetts, 1936.

Gilman, Daniel C., ed. *Organization of Charities: Report of the 6th Section of the International Congress of Charities.* Baltimore, 1894.

———. *The Launching of a University.* New York, 1906.

Greenleaf, Robert W. *An Historical Report of the Boston Dispensary for One Hundred Years: 1796–1896.* Brookline, Massachusetts, 1898.

Halbert, L. A. *What is Professional Social Work?* New York, 1923.

Handlin, Oscar. *Boston's Immigrants.* Cambridge, Massachusetts, 1959.

Higham, John. *Strangers in the Land.* New Brunswick, New Jersey, 1955.

Hofstadter, Richard. *Social Darwinism in American Thought.* New York, 1959.

Hopkins, Charles H. *The Rise of the Social Gospel in American Protestantism, 1865–1915.* New Haven, Connecticut, 1940.

Howe, Mark A. DeW. *The Humane Society of the Commonwealth of Massachusetts.* 2 vols. Cambridge, Massachusetts, 1918.

———. *Memories of a Hostess.* Boston, 1922.

James, Henry. *The American Scene.* New York, 1907.

Johnson, Alexander. *Adventures in Social Welfare.* Fort Wayne, Indiana, 1923.

Kelso, Robert W. *The History of Public Poor Relief in Massachusetts, 1620–1920.* Boston, 1922.

Lane, Roger. *Policing the City: Boston, 1822–1885.* Cambridge, Massachusetts, 1967.

Leiby, James. *Carroll Wright and Labor Reform.* Cambridge, Massachusetts, 1960.

Lord, Robert H. and Sexton, John E. *History of the Arch-Diocese of Boston.* 3 vols. Boston, 1944.

Lubove, Roy. *The Professional Altruist; the Emergence of Social Work as a Career, 1880–1930.* Cambridge, Massachusetts, 1965.

Lynn, Kenneth S., ed. *The Professions in America.* Boston, 1965.

Mann, Arthur. *Yankee Reformers in an Urban Age.* Cambridge, Massachusetts, 1954.

Mark, Kenneth L. *Delayed by Fire, Being the Early History of Simmons College.* Concord, New Hampshire, 1945.

May, Henry F. *Protestant Churches and Industrial America.* New York, 1949.

McColgan, Daniel T. *Joseph Tuckerman.* Washington, D.C., 1940.

Meier, Elizabeth G. *A History of the New York School of Social Work.* New York, 1954.

Niebuhr, H. Richard. *The Kingdom of God in America.* Chicago, 1937.

Olmstead, Clifton E. *History of Religion in the United States.* Englewood Cliffs, New Jersey, 1960.

Paine, Sarah Cushing, comp. *Paine Ancestry.* Boston, 1912.

Parker, Ida R. *"Fit and Proper?" A Study of Legal Adoption in Massachusetts.* Boston, 1927.

Patten, Simon N. *The New Basis of Civilization.* Edited by Daniel M. Fox. Cambridge, Massachusetts, 1968.

Persons, Stow, ed. *Evolutionary Thought in America.* New Haven, 1950.

Pumphrey, Ralph E. and Muriel W., eds. *The Heritage of American Social Work.* New York, 1961.

Solomon, Barbara Miller. *Ancestors and Immigrants.* Cambridge, Massachusetts, 1956.

———. *Pioneers in Service.* Boston, 1956.

Sumner, William G. *Essays of William Graham Sumner.* Edited by A. G. Keller and M. R. Davie. Vol 1. New Haven, 1934.

Sweet, William W. *The Story of Religion in America.* New York, 1939.

Tawney, R. H. *Religion and the Rise of Capitalism.* New York, 1952.

Thurston, Henry W. *The Dependent Child.* New York, 1930.

Warner, Amos G. *American Charities.* New York, 1894.

Washburn, Frederick A. *The Massachusetts General Hospital.* Boston, 1939.

Watson, Frank D. *The Charity Organization Movement in the United States.* New York, 1922.

Weber, Max. *The Protestant Ethic and the Spirit of Capitalism.* Translated by Talcott Parsons. New York, 1958.

Whitehill, Walter Muir. *Boston, a Topographical History.* Cambridge, Massachusetts, 1959.

Whiteside, William B. *The Boston Y.M.C.A. and Community Need.* New York, 1951.

Williams, Melvin J. *Catholic Social Thought.* New York, 1950.

Willoughby, William F. *State Activities in Relation to Labor in the United States.* Baltimore, 1901.

Winsor, Justin, ed. *The Memorial History of Boston, 1630–1880.* Vol. IV. Boston, 1886.

Wolfe, Albert B. *The Lodging House Problem in Boston.* Boston, 1906.

Zollmann, Carl. *American Law of Charities.* Milwaukee, Wisconsin, 1924.

ARTICLES

Bernstein, Barton J. "Francis Greenwood Peabody: Conservative Social Reformer." *New England Quarterly* XXXVI (Spring 1963), pp. 320–337.

Curti, Merle, "American Philanthropy and the National Character." *The American Quarterly* X (Winter 1958), pp. 420–437.

Griffin, Clifford S. "Religious Benevolence as Social Control, 1815–1860." *The Mississippi Valley Historical Review* XLIV (December 1957), pp. 423–444.

James, Henry. "Mr. & Mrs. James T. Fields." *The Atlantic Monthly* CXVI (July 1915), pp. 21–31.

Index

DATE DUE

OCT. 0 5 1992 SEP 24 '92			
GAYLORD			PRINTED IN U.S.A.